Michael Eastman OBE has been Sec[...] for Urban Mission since its formatic [...] 31 years as Chief Executive of Frontier Youth Trust. He served as an adviser to the Archbishop's Commission on Urban Priority Areas, which produced the *Faith in the City* report. A member of the Editorial Board of *Urban Bulletin*, his published writing includes *Ten Inner City Churches* (Kingsway, 1988), which he edited.

Steve Latham is Pastor of Westbourne Park Baptist Church in Paddington, west London. Before that he was Pastor of Downs Baptist Church in Hackney. He has a PhD in contemporary prophetic ministry from King's College, London. He is married to Sue and has two children, Joanna and Michael.

Urban Church

A practitioner's resource book

Edited by

Michael Eastman

and

Steve Latham

First published in Great Britain in 2004 by
Society for Promoting Christian Knowledge
Holy Trinity Church
Marylebone Road
London NW1 4DU

Unless otherwise designated, Scripture quotations are taken from the
HOLY BIBLE, NEW INTERNATIONAL VERSION, copyright © 1973,
1978, 1984 by International Bible Society. Used by permission of Hodder
& Stoughton Ltd, a member of Hodder Headline Plc Group.
Scripture quotations marked GNB are from the Good News Bible
published by The Bible Societies/HarperCollins Publishers Ltd UK
© American Bible Society, 1966, 1971, 1976, 1992, 1994.

British Library Cataloguing-in-Publication Data
A catalogue record for this book is available from the British Library.

ISBN 0-281-05603-X

1 3 5 7 9 10 8 6 4 2

Designed and typeset by Kenneth Burnley, Wirral, Cheshire
Printed in Malta by Gutenberg

Contents

Introduction   vii
Evangelical Coalition for Urban Mission   x

1 **Beginning to Think**   1
   The Story of Urban Mission in the UK   *Colin Marchant*   2
   Doing Theology in the Urban Context   *Kenneth Leech*   5
   Key Biblical Themes   *Colin Marchant*   8

2 **Church Life**   12
   The Importance of Being Church   *Steve Latham*   13
   Building a Community   *Kofi Manful*   16
   Local Church Leadership in Urban Communities   *Jim Hart*   19
   New Models of Church   *Stuart Murray Williams*   22

3 **Spirituality and Worship**   26
   Maintaining Hope: How to Keep Going and Not
      Burn Out   *Chris Burch*   27
   Worship: Making it Real in the City?   *Pete Hobson*   30
   Urban Worship   *Jacqueline Brown*   33
   Worship Alternatives: Use of Arts and Creativity in
      Worship   *Doug Gay*   36

4 **Scripture**   40
   Bible Study: The Liberation Theology Method
      John Vincent   41
   Unlocking Real Life!   *Jenny Richardson*   45
   Preaching in an Urban World   *Roger Sainsbury*   49

5 **Community**   53
   Building Community: Within and Without the Walls
      of the Church   *Greg Smith*   54
   Community Development   *Chris Erskine*   57
   'On' the Estate   *Andy Dorton*   60
   Political Involvement: Local Resistance to Regeneration
      Policies   *Alan Craig*   63

6 Race 68
The Multicultural Society, the Multicultural Church
Wale Hudson Roberts 69
'I Was a Stranger' Sheila Garvin 71
Look: A Multicultural Church! Andy Bruce 74
Planting a Chinese Congregation in Hounslow:
A Decade of Mission Robert Tang 77

7 Cultural Change 82
Pluralism and Diversity Graham Routley 83
An Incomer's Tale Mark Perrott 86
Searching for Roots: Power and Powerlessness
Richard Springer 89
Recent Arrivals Wagih Abdelmassih 92

8 Peace-making 96
The 174 Story Patton Taylor 97
Race in Northern Towns: Christian Responses to
BNP–Muslim Tensions Geoff Reid 100
Gang Violence Paul Keeble 103
In the Congregation Tim Foley 106

9 Some Other Urban Issues 111
A Healthy Living Project in a Local Church
Simon Standen 112
Debt Bob Holman 114
Work: Toxteth Tabernacle Baptist Church/Toxteth
Vine Project Terry Jones 117
Employment Dave Rogers 120

10 Faith-sharing 124
Urban Mission Derek Purnell 125
Evangelism in a Multifaith Setting Amanda Gray 128
Urban Cell Church Howard Astin 132
Church Planting Juliet Kilpin 137

Further Reading 141
Agencies, Networks and Resources 147

Introduction

Jesus loved the city. He longed that she would experience the shalom-peace of his kingdom and wept when she rejected it (Luke 19.41–2). In the Old Testament, Jeremiah wrote to the exiles in Babylon that they were to pray for and work for the shalom-peace wholeness and prosperity of that enemy city (Jeremiah 29.7).

Urban mission would seem then to be a priority for the Christian Church. Indeed many women and men, both those employed by the Church as congregational leaders and community workers, have worked selflessly in the inner cities and outer estates. Some have served as individuals in secular or local community organizations; others have done so from a base in the local congregation. Both are expressions of the corporate life of the Body of Christ in its gathered and dispersed forms.

The year 2005 will be the twentieth anniversary of the report *Faith in the City*, which highlighted the need for Christian witness in the inner cities during the Thatcher era. There were, rightly, many criticisms of that report on political and theological grounds. Although it was more reformist than radical, many of its recommendations have still not been implemented. The 1980s also saw the founding of the Evangelical Coalition of Urban Mission, while in 1998 the Church of England Lambeth Conference launched the Anglican Urban Network.

Recently, urban mission has slipped further down the ecclesiastical agenda. The numerical and institutional decline of the Church has led to a one-sided concentration on management and on 'what works', a preoccupation with institutional survival rather than mission. In addition, financial problems due to economic mismanagement in the Church and other factors have encouraged a monetarist short-termism, which favours growing suburban churches over costly incarnational ministry in Urban Priority Areas (UPAs). Denominations and para-church organizations have cut funding and programmes which relate to our concerns. At the same time, problems in the inner cities and outer estates continue to worsen. Regeneration policies do not make much of a dent, and sometimes make things worse. Furthermore, the problems usually associated with UPAs are now found throughout the country, as urbanization spreads social and lifestyle trends even to the suburbs.

The year 2004 sees the fourth UK Urban Mission Congress – Jesus in the City of Glasgow. This and other gatherings represent opportunities to raise the profile of urban mission. A recent issue of *Anvil* was wholly devoted to urban theology, and that doyen of urban mission,[1] Laurie Green, has just written a considered examination of urban ministry.[2] Perhaps we are on a rising tide of urban rediscovery among Christians, a second wind.

This book contributes something unique – a series of short snapshots from practitioners. The collection includes story-telling and theological reflection. Some articles emphasize one more than the other. Some are personal and deeply moving, others studied and reflective. Some give practical information and insight, others are inspirational and exciting. You will see that there is a great variety in the situations and perspectives represented here. Some are stories of change amidst the rapidly changing flux and flow of the cityscape. There are accounts of experimentation as well as faithful long-term service. There is also sometimes anger and frustration at the disappointments and strain of urban ministry. There is therefore, inevitably, a calling into question of what is stereotypically considered 'effective' or 'successful' ministry or mission. The results of urban mission do not often translate into the quantifiable, *positive* 'outputs' and 'outcomes' required by funders.

There are contributors who stress the importance of practical, hands-on help for local people, whether from the Church base or through other community projects. Others emphasize prophetic, political resistance to, and questioning of, ecclesiastical priorities and government policies. Many of the examples are of small initiatives. All illustrate the need for long-term, sustained commitment to a community in order to see transformation. Some of the contributors certainly will not agree with each other! This is because as we each wrestle with the demands of contextualizing our faith, the influences of the person as well as the place will interact to produce a unique view. Contextual theology is inevitably micro-theology. The resulting picture is of incredible diversity and complexity. Urban mission cannot be reduced to a single formula. There are no easy answers. We have therefore included, at the end of each chapter, a set of questions; and there is a list of resources and books in a section at the back, to guide readers in their further reflection.

We realize, of course, that this is not a complete picture of urban mission in the UK. These stories and articles are tasters. There are many gaps; we have, for example, no Roman Catholic contributions, where they are perhaps on the cutting edge of incarnational justice and welfare ministries in many of our urban areas. In addition, we recognize that there is a relative lack of contributions from women and people from ethnic minorities. Both of these are serious shortcomings in our book. Ethnic congregations are among the fastest growing in our cities, and exemplify much of the energy and dynamism of the urban Church. Women, moreover, are among the poorest of city dwellers, but also critically key to much of the Christian life, community and congregational, in our cities. These and all other inadequacies in our book are wholly our own fault, due often to a lack of contacts and pressure of time. We apologize.

We thank the Evangelical Coalition for Urban Mission for encouraging the production of this book, and our publishers, SPCK, for having the courage to publish it. Finally, we are deeply grateful to all our contributors who have worked hard to get articles in by the deadlines. They have written a body of work which seriously contributes to the knowledge and experience of urban mission in the UK. We acknowledge the depth of their thinking and the cost of their commitment to God's kingdom in the city.

MICHAEL EASTMAN AND STEVE LATHAM

Notes

1 *Anvil*, Vol. 20, No. 2 (2003).
2 Laurie Green, *Urban Ministry and the Kingdom of God* (SPCK, 2003).

Evangelical Coalition for Urban Mission

Founded in 1980 and launched the following year, ECUM is a coalition of Christian agencies working with others for the well-being (shalom) of inner urban industrial areas and outer estates, together working for the transformation of our cities according to God's purposes as set out in the Bible. The current work of ECUM includes:

- Organizing the Urban Mission Forum to provide support of urban mission practice.
- Convening the Network of Urban Evangelicals, an annual gathering of representatives from Christian agencies engaged in urban mission.
- Publishing *Urban Reflection* (incorporating *City Cries*), a twice-yearly comprehensive information service covering urban mission issues, publications, resources, events, news and comment.
- Providing advice and resources for those engaged in urban issues of ministry.
- Running training events and courses.
- Liaising with a wide range of others within the UK and internationally in this field.

The present partners of ECUM are:

Frontier Youth Trust.
Unlock (formerly Evangelical Urban Training Project).
CURBS (Children in Urban Situations).
Worth Unlimited.
Scripture Union's Urban and Justice Ministries.
Urban Vision (formerly Ministry Amongst Asians in Britain) – a ministry of Interserve.
Crusaders.

For further details contact ECUM's National Office at 305 Cambridge Heath Road, London E2 9LH; phone: 020 7729 6262; fax: 020 7739 5079; e-mail: ecum1@tiscali.co.uk

1

Beginning to Think

In this first chapter we include three contributions which illustrate some of the foundational ideas. They give us tools we can use in our thinking about urban mission.

Colin Marchant describes some of the major waves of urban mission in the UK, and helps us situate ourselves in this wider story. No matter what we feel from time to time, we are not alone! We are part of God's history in the city.

Kenneth Leech shows us how urban theology is a contextual theology, and must be rooted by the experience of long-term living and working in a community.

Finally, **Colin Marchant** gives an account of the main biblical motifs which regularly and repeatedly crop up when urban practitioners begin to talk about what resources they find in the Word of God.

The Story of Urban Mission in the UK

Colin Marchant

Baptist minister and training consultant on urban mission
in east London

Start where you are

Look around you. The efforts and styles of urban mission and
ministry are embedded in buildings, people and records. Parish
church or mission hall, community centre or shopfront. Buildings
abandoned, adapted or recycled. Each carrying a message, expressing a theology or telling a story.

Talk to the people: individuals or families giving continuity or
change; incomers or immigrants bringing different cultures and
faiths. Turn out the records: local newspapers and church magazines, tombstones and lists, census records and membership
statistics. Reflect as you street-walk, listen as others tell their story,
jot down facts as you read. You are journeying through local faith
history.

You are not alone: your district has been touched by the movements of urban mission that have spread across the UK.
Long-established Anglican churches, Catholic convents and mon-
asteries, and Free Church chapels stand alongside church schools,
almshouses and vicarages in pastoral and educational presence. But
swirling around them is the evidence of changing patterns, initiatives
and movements that make up urban mission history. Layer after
layer, wave after wave.

Missions, agencies, armies, settlements, Central Halls

City Missions began in Glasgow in 1826 and spread rapidly to
Bristol, Belfast, Liverpool, Edinburgh, London, Leeds and Manchester. A second wave started in 1966 with Birmingham, Coventry,
Derby and Bradford following on. Missioners, halls, tracts, personal
evangelism, patch-working and people groups were key features
with hands-on and practical ministries.

Agencies proliferated in the Victorian era. The YMCA, Shaftesbury Society and Society of St Vincent de Paul all started in 1844.
Work among children alone led to Barnardo's (founded in 1870),
Muller's Homes, the Catholic Children's Society, Spurgeon's Child-
care, National Children's Homes, Fegans and the Children's Society

in the late 1880s. Local, regional and national agencies with Christian roots operate across the UK, many continuing, adapting or diversifying their work.

Armies appeared first in London. William Booth launched the Salvation Army in 1865. Uniforms, military discipline, brass bands, open-air meetings, citadels and temples created both a new religious community and an evangelistic agency that soon moved into social care. The Church Army's first press notice in 1882 read:

> The Church Army has commenced at Walworth. Its nightly procession, consisting of a clergyman with a banner, half a dozen lady workers and a number of laity, has been pelted with cabbage stumps and rotten apples.

These evangelical armies matched the Anglican and Catholic orders who were already moving into the big cities with mission and ministry based in convent and monastery and expressed in education, health and compassion. Uniformed organizations in the Boys' Brigade and Girls' Brigade followed on in 1883 and 1893.

Settlements began in east London with Toynbee Hall in 1884, and by 1913 there were 45. Public schools and universities were behind the School Missions and Settlements that funded work or sent groups of students to live among the poor and initiate an extensive range of social activities. Oxford House and St Margaret's House echo the past links but most Settlements are now social action centres.

The Methodist *Central Halls/Missions* took Methodism's urban concern to the heart of UK cities and large towns. By 1919 there were 41. In 1900 the Manchester Mission had more than 14,000 people in 12 branches. Traditional styles of worship and evangelism moved to a wide programme of education, entertainment, ministry and outreach centred in large buildings with a big staff.

Communities and industrial mission

The devastating impact of two world wars, the emergence of the Labour Party in the late 1890s and changing industrial processes drew the churches into different responses. Much established work carried on in the churches, missions and agencies right through the years 1900 to 1950.

Intentional and dispersed *communities* began to emerge as a focus and forum. In Scotland the Iona Community, founded by George

MacLeod in 1938, focused on new ways of living the gospel. Later, at Corrymeela, another dispersed Christian community worked to break down barriers and build bridges in Northern Ireland. In England, the William Temple Foundation, now in Manchester, began 'action research and training in urban industrial mission and community action'.

Industrial mission began in Sheffield in 1944 and moved on from the earlier efforts of the Missions and the Industrial Christian Fellowship to become a highly organized and professional network of chaplains and teams. The Sheffield Industrial Mission, Luton Industrial College and the South London Industrial Mission were, by 1978, at the heart of 373 chaplains in 40 English city or diocesan teams. Scotland had 100 part-time chaplains in ten teams and Wales had 19 full-timers in four teams.

Networks, projects
In the 1960s urban Christians began to 'join hands' and to earth their work in housing estates, new towns and inner cities. Immigrants now lived among the white working class. The Ecumenical and the Charismatic movements were with us.

Networks of the involved or concerned began to emerge. Newsletters like *Christians in Industrial Areas* led on to the later *City Cries* and *Urban Bulletin*. Training initiatives ranged from the Urban Theology Unit based in Sheffield and the Evangelical Urban Training Programme (now Unlock) in Liverpool. Concern for young people emerged in the Frontier Youth Trust and Youth with a Mission.

In the 1970s and 1980s came the emphasis on poverty with Church Action on Poverty and the evidence of a 'reverse missionary flow' in the Asian Christian Fellowship and the Afro-Caribbean Evangelical Council together with the Black and White Partnership in Birmingham. Groups like Jubilee and NACCAN (National Association of Community Centres and Networks) ran alongside ECUM (Evangelical Coalition for Urban Mission).

But it was two denominations that lifted urban mission to a high national profile. The launch of the Methodist Mission Alongside the Poor in 1983 led into a wide range of projects based on churches across the country, many in multiracial areas. The Anglican *Faith in the City* report of 1985 hit the headlines and galvanized the churches. The follow-through Church Urban Fund made possible hundreds of projects in urban priority areas.

GLO-CAL

Moving towards the millennium in the 1990s urban mission and ministry experienced a renewed emphasis on the local and the invigorating impact of global movements of people. The two great waves of urban mission at the close of each century, Victorian and Elizabethan, had left a legacy of buildings, organizations, writings and stories alongside the congregations set in the urban area.

Now the GLObal–loCAL era is with us comprising ethnic congregations from African and Asian nations. Multifaith, internationally linked religions, different cultures and languages – all are evident in our urban sprawls. Another piece of urban mission and ministry history is being written.

Overview and benchmarks

We can look back to see the initiatives, trends and efforts within the first nation to face the Industrial Revolution. Each named group represents many others. They are benchmarks for the urban journey in the UK which is now accelerating. Those who read this can identify, uncover and learn from the past which is now in the present and moving towards the future story of urban mission and ministry in the United Kingdom.

Doing Theology in the Urban Context

Kenneth Leech
Community theologian working at St Botolph's Church, Aldgate, east London

For the last 13 years I have been employed as a 'community theologian' based at an east London church. What does this mean? At a simplistic level, I am nothing more or less than a theologian who has chosen to work within a geographical neighbourhood rather than within academia. However, to do theological work outside of a community which both recognizes it as a discrete discipline and compartmentalizes it within certain boundaries means that both the process and the methodology are bound to shift. Some of the shifts are the result of the environment, the context, while others are the result of reflection and struggle, personal and corporate. As theology comes into contact and collision with its context, it is bound to change its character and style.

In 1990 at St Botolph's Church, Aldgate, we decided that it was important to employ a theologian, a member of the team whose primary activity was to pray, reflect and think – not on behalf of others or instead of them, but in co-operation with them, and to contribute to the work of theological reflection within the Christian community in this area. We felt that it was very easy for local churches to avoid serious thinking, and simply to carry on doing what they had always done. It seemed particularly dangerous for us, working in the field of homelessness, to operate a crisis ministry, binding up the wounded and responding to one urgent need after another, but never to make the time to reflect on what it was all about, what it had to do with the gospel, what the wider social and political issues were, and what God was up to in the struggles and upheavals which confronted us.

I should add two important aspects of this decision. First, while the original idea was mine, the decision was made by all the workers in both the church and the crypt project. Had there not been this common mind – a close working relationship between the worshipping community and those employed to work with homeless people – I would not have felt it right to begin the theology work.

Second, we had no money, and realized that 'doing theology in Whitechapel Road' was not exactly 'fundogenic'! Raising the money, with the accompanying need for regular documentation, scrutiny and accountability, has been an essential part of the work.

The focus of the work remains as it was in 1990, though much has changed in the area and in the life of the local church. There are three aspects to my work. First, to develop theological thinking and action in the fields of drug abuse, homelessness and racial justice: building on work which I had been doing on these issues in the East End for over 30 years. So the theology began with concrete issues. Second, to link the local with the global, to connect the work at St Botolph's with wider networks of thought, with the Church beyond Aldgate, and with social and political issues nationally and internationally. Third, to pursue theological reflection from the context of inner east London, and to make links with the growing numbers of people in many different places who have chosen to do their theology mainly outside the academic world. The immediate context of my work is the area between Aldgate and Stepney, going north to the border of Hackney and south to Shadwell.

Theology is, in a literal sense, 'a word about God', 'a word of God', or 'God talk'. But it has come to mean something abstruse, archaic, out of date and out of touch, irrelevant, entirely theoretical. Christians are not entirely free of blame for this. Yet for Christians theology is of critical importance, for it is about trying to make sense of what God is up to in the world, and in our specific context, and how we co-operate with it rather than hinder it.

What does this mean in terms of how we do theology at the local level? Seven elements seem to me to be important in the light of my experience in east London.

First, each small local Christian community is the locus for theological activity. In Bob Schreiter's terms, the community is a theologian. This means that more theological work will be done within groups than by individuals working in isolation. We have had small groups working theologically on issues such as dying, death and bereavement; the meaning of community; introductions to contemporary theologians; theology and organized racism; and so on.

Second, this activity need not only be an intellectual one, though undoubtedly the intellect will be involved. But theology involves other human responses; and poetry, art, music, and so on can be forms of theological expression. One Lent we hung an enormous painting – 'Scene of a Crucifixion with Seven Deadly Sins' by the Irish artist Brian Breathnach – behind the High Altar, and framed all our sermons and reflections around the issues it raised. I have recently led several retreats using the remarkable 'Stations of the Cross' by Beverley Barr (formerly from the East End) in Christ Church, Eastbourne.

Third, theological work must involve a cross-section of people in terms of age, class, culture, and so on. Donald Nicholl once said that theology should never be done without the presence of children. Theology changes as the participants change, and as the base is broadened. People who do not know the jargon or the etiquette often undermine and shift the whole focus of the discussion.

Fourth, theological work is an ongoing activity. It does not have a clear end point. It involves continual interrogation, questing, struggling, wrestling. It is not a closed system.

Fifth, theology is messy. It is confronted by issues and crises – in the world, in the parish, in the neighbourhood, and in our own personal lives – to which it does not have simple and clear answers. It has therefore to live with mess and incompleteness. This does not mean that the quest for clarity is a mistake: only that it does not all come at once! Thomas Aquinas famously saw his enormous output as straw compared with the vision of God.

Sixth, prayer is central, and without a prayerful, contemplative base, the whole activity fails. As Evagrius said in the fourth century, 'a theologian is one whose prayer is true'. Or, as Rowan Williams said recently, 'the subject of theology is a person who prays'.

Finally, theology does involve belief, for it is concerned with truth. Alasdair MacIntyre complained that liberal theologians were giving atheists 'less and less in which to disbelieve'. The justified reaction against fundamentalisms and forms of religious arrogance cannot lie in the abandonment of truth claims. Jesus told us that we shall know the truth, and the truth shall make us free, and this must remain central to the task of the local church.

Key Biblical Themes

Colin Marchant
Baptist minister and training consultant on urban mission
in east London

Urban Mission has buzz words, many of which echo Scripture. 'Kingdom', 'servant', 'poor' and 'shalom' run through the Bible. 'Incarnation', 'justice' and 'mission' are foundation stones in the building of any ministry or project in urban areas. Key-note words and themes recur often and are repeated frequently. Among us they are recognized and act as both root and resource.

Begin with mission

Start with Jesus. He gives the mandate for all mission in the Great Commission of Matthew 28.16–20: 'Go into all the world.' He sets out a manifesto in Luke 4.16–20 that clearly embraces the poor, prisoner, blind and oppressed: the marginalized of our day. And by his life and teaching he gives the model for what we call the holistic gospel.

Tune into the key-notes

Incarnation is primary: being there; embedded; in the flesh. 'Making the Word flesh' is set out in John 1.1–14. The steps of God–servant–human–humbled–obedient–cross of Philippians 2.5–11 precede lifted–name–every knee–every tongue–Jesus is Lord. That's why disciples are told to be salt or light in their communities. Belong and being, carrying and feeling, part of . . . that's incarnation.

Servant follows. It is the style of all ministry and mission. Jesus lived with the 'servant songs' of Isaiah. The disciples are clearly shown and taught (look at Mark 10.41–5) that others come first and that power-play is not the way. Every time we talk about ministry or service we use both the language and the message of the Bible.

Shalom is central. This is the Bible's word for salvation, justice and peace. It means whole, complete, at one. Although it is usually translated as 'peace' it is much more. This is the purpose of the shalom-God for the individual, relationships, church, community, nation and world. Check it out for yourself in Numbers 6.24–6, Ephesians 1.14–18, Psalm 122 and Colossians 1.20. That's why we are to seek the shalom-welfare of the city of Jeremiah 29.7 and to share in 'the Peace' in our congregations.

Kingdom is the vision word. This is a 'way of speaking about God's work within human time and history'. The word occurs 121 times in Scripture. In Jesus 'the kingdom of God is near' and we all pray 'your kingdom come'. Everywhere and in every situation God has both a presence and a purpose – housing estate or inner city, individual or community, local or global. Because the kingdom is both here and yet to come we are all in the business of struggle and transformation.

Be held by the themes that resonate in the urban of today
Never lose the *value of the individual* within the anonymity or change of the city. 'Made in the likeness of God', 'For you', prodigal son, good Samaritan, dying thief, leper: it's all in the Bible! You

heard it for yourself. It is to be carried to others. Frail elderly, asylum-seeker, drug addict, stranger, ordinary folk. Love, compassion, acceptance, time, welcome.

Face the poor: the Bible does. Over 300 references reveal a broad understanding of the causes, reality and consequences of poverty. The poor person is downtrodden, humiliated, oppressed; burdened, powerless and needy. This poverty causes concern, anger and protest. It is challenged and opposed in the Scriptures. Its source is seen as injustice and oppression by the powerful. God is on their side. Jesus invites the poor. From the UK urban has sprung Church Action on Poverty, and in the daily work of mission there must be 'Good news for the poor'.

That will bring you to a cluster of themes in *justice*, *jubilee*, *liberation*. God is just and he wills justice. His prophets expose legalized oppression. 'Jubilee' is a rediscovered word with the fundamental idea of release as it enters into the world of debt, possessions, property and economics (plenty of that in the urban!).

Liberation springs from the 'Let my people go' of the Old Testament and the 'being set free' of the New and is contemporary in liberation theology. This is all pictured in the thread of the kinsman-intervener or Go-el (translated as 'redeemer') that runs through the Old Testament. Exodus deliverance is a vital thread running through both testaments.

You will certainly have to wrestle with *principalities and powers*. Evil in its reality, power and pervasiveness in the satanic forces and hidden control that we call 'structural sin' and know in our own bitter experience. Paul's call to 'spiritual warfare' in Ephesians 6.10–18 and the temptations of Jesus recorded in Luke 4.1–13 are a must, especially for the professionals and politicians.

City has a double dimension in the Bible. There are 119 different cities named and there are 1,600 references in the Old Testament and 119 in the New Testament to cities and city living in the social, cultural and religious systems. But Jerusalem (foundation-shalom) is to be the City of God where God's will and way are kept and his glory seen. That is why Jesus enters, weeps and judges the city of Jerusalem and goes on to make possible the vision of the heavenly, final city set out in Revelation 21.

Mission in the complexity and tangle of the urban will bring us again and again to the *cross* and *resurrection*. Paul prayed from Philippi, 'I want to know Christ and the power of his resurrection and the fellowship of sharing in his sufferings'. Hurt and healing, silence and singing, sin and forgiveness, death and new life: it's all there. And you will find it – the great signs stand. And there are others that you discover for yourself or receive from others. 'Journey', 'spirit', 'discipleship', 'exile', 'creation', 'covenant' and 'grace' are among them. All are key words that open understanding and sustain the 'going on' in the work of urban mission and ministry.

Questions for Further Thought and Action

1 Map the churches in your locality. Find out their vision and what they are currently doing. What do they owe to the past? How do they see the future?

2 Bring together a group which will develop a local theology under-girding the vision and practice of your church.

3 Colin Marchant's checklist:
   (a) Get a Bible with cross references or a concordance.
   (b) Live with the *overview*. Snippets and sections are known. Get the flow.
   (c) Watch *selectivity* – we know and like some things, ignore and refuse others.
   (d) Guard against *spiritualization* – keeping the words but changing the meaning, e.g. 'shalom' often shrinks now to 'inner peace', and salvation becomes purely personal.

2

Church Life

In this chapter we look at the formation and re-formation of the people of God in the city. We examine the importance of their common life, as the community of God's kingdom. The contributions stress that this is not identical with the traditional forms of church life in the UK, and indeed may at times militate against these inherited structures. In particular, the Church must adapt to the experience of an urban life, which often disperses and disaggregates, making difficult any expression of communal relationships. How can we draw people together into a corporate life, when so much pulls them apart, separating them into isolated flats and ghettoized sub-cultures?

Steve Latham tells how his experience of community action led him to appreciate the role of the corporate people of God in promoting and supporting social change.

Kofi Manful explains the particular contribution of the pastor in constructing the local congregation as a community, encouraging supportive and caring relationships among members.

Jim Hart questions the imprisonment of Church in tradition and seeks for ways of empowering working-class people as authentic leaders of their congregations through encountering the Word.

Finally, **Stuart Murray Williams** examines some of the experimentation being carried out into new forms of 'doing Church': new ways of being together, which relate to our urban context.

The Importance of Being Church

Steve Latham

Pastor at Westbourne Park Baptist Church, Paddington, London

I came to London to be a youth and community worker on a council housing estate. We ran the usual youth clubs, but also worked with residents to set up a Tenants' Association. This group lobbied the council to get improvements. But when I left the project (the youth clubs having erupted in violence and my flat having been burgled four times in six weeks!), the only physical changes were some traffic bollards and a tiny playground. Ten years later the promised refurbishment of the flats was still unfinished, with scaffolding covering several blocks. And when I finally moved back into the area, after another five years, the work was still incomplete amid rumours of ten million pounds going astray.

The experience left me convinced of the need for a committed community of faith, to be the focus for community organization and change. I had come in as a 'Lone Ranger' urban missionary called to save the inner city. I was motivated by Jesus' Nazareth Manifesto (Luke 4.18–19). But I interpreted it in a heroic mould. I realized eventually I could not do it alone – only with God and his people.

My experience mirrored the felt powerlessness of many inner-city people in the face of council bureaucracies and commercial interests. Frequently I find local people have no social body to which they belong: families have disintegrated, voluntary groups collapsed, and national organizations departed. Often too the churches have given up the (Holy) Spirit.

Community

But my experience is that Church can provide a sense of belonging, a body to join, a cause, God's kingdom project. It is attractive, and when people see it in action (through kids' clubs, debt counselling, unemployment projects, playgroups), and where they are welcomed by a caring, inclusive, open congregation, then they want to identify with what God is doing among them.

Church is community, and builds wider community. The Church-as-community can contribute to the welfare of the community-as-neighbourhood (Jeremiah 29.7), when we identify the 'man of peace' (Matthew 10.11), the people of goodwill, with whom to work. At the same time, Church is an alternative community, posing a prophetic challenge and witness to our neighbours about how to live.

It's a mistake therefore to think the Church can be the 'centre' of the community. We shall always be 'eccentric' – just off-centre, marching to the beat of a different drum, pointing the way. The Church is a pilot project of the future-in-the-present, modelling relationships lived out in God's Spirit.

Church is important because it can form an organizational base, to administer community initiatives and attract funds. We need strong urban institutions. Sceptical Christian radicals seem to suspect anything institutional. But to deal with the powers of this world, we need an alternative power base, a counter-cultural stronghold (2 Corinthians 10.4). This world, of tower blocks, regeneration developments, poverty and racism, is not yet God's kingdom. It is coming, but for now we are in a battle zone (Ephesians 6.12).

Church also compensates for the weakness of projects. Community projects are always short-lived. Church can provide longevity, an organizational base which will be there for the long haul. Grants dry up. Professional community activists have little commitment to the neighbourhood in which they operate. What matters to them is their career and mobility. Instead of hiring outsiders, we must equip local people as leaders in church and community (Ephesians 4.11–12).

Criticisms

Are there not criticisms to make of the Church? Of course. There is degeneration, deformation. Churches can be alienating, unwelcoming, rejecting, centres of power not Pentecost, cold buildings not warm communities. But the Church is still the Bride of Christ (Revelation 19.7), the first-fruits of the New Creation (James 1.18).

This does not mean the superstructure of Church, with its hierarchy and tradition, whether from the twelfth, seventeenth or nineteenth century. In the urban, Church will have to adapt its missionary form to the styles of the *oppidum*. The few believers meeting in their flat for fellowship are as much 'Church' as the liturgical, priestified gathering on a Sunday in the sacred building (Acts 2.46). The styles of urban Church have to change, as our youth say, for the 'Churban'.

It will break out and wash over the steep banks of our inherited traditions, and empower people to lead their own churches. We do not need the clergy caste to direct us but fire and passion; the anointing. Popular movements of the Spirit move from deconstruction to construction. We do not yet see what he will produce. But we do see he blends the spiritual and the social. Intercession and community action join in practice rather than through theory, as disciples do both.

Christians

To affect our neighbourhoods, we need Church. But to build Church, we need disciples. Without Christians, we cannot have Christian community action. So we need to ask, where are these Christians going to come from? After all, the Church is shrinking. And we cannot keep depending parasitically in Britain on the reinforcements from immigration – which is the main reason why the London inner-city churches are still surviving.

We need to make more Christians! Reproduction. This means evangelism – proactive, deliberate and planned. Not pulling punches. Recruiting people for God's kingdom project to change, if not the whole world, as least our part of it, our estate (Mark 1.14–18). Not separating proclamation and demonstration, but calling people to a radical lifestyle and belonging to God's new community even in the midst of the old which is passing away (Romans 8.11–12).

Then we need to think about nurture, for those who respond in faith and those brought up in the faith: a systematic and structured programme of instruction in the language of faith. Not the prompting of theological cynicism but the passing on of spiritual certainties to nourish them through the trials and tribulations of debt, illness or unemployment.

For this we must counter the individualism of contemporary consumerism, which discourages commitment to any body of people, but which encourages mobility, leisure and shopping. Today many Christians drop out of church, through spiritual disillusionment, political distrust or personal rejection. We must call them back to the cause of God's kingdom, lived in relationship with other misfits, nobodies and sad cases (1 Corinthians 1.26–9).

It's precisely this bunch whom we meet around the Lord's Supper that constitutes Church, the 'light of the world' (Matthew 5.14). This celebration is the high note of our witness: rejoicing over the future-in-the-present; enjoying relationships. Urban congregations eat together lots! Let's invite others to the party by having real parties (Matthew 22.1–14).

Building a Community

Kofi Manful
Pastor at Faith Baptist Church, Tottenham, London

To create a biblical community in the Church we must wrestle with *koinonia*. This Greek word, translated 'fellowship', is a relationship word. It shows Christians the authentic fellowship we have in Christ. The Church is expected to meet the basic human needs of friendship and fellowship. Our goal in Faith Baptist Church is to be a church where everybody is somebody, where everybody is valued, cherished, loved and respected. To model such an attractive and visible vision of community does not happen automatically. Let us look at three factors that can help us to create biblical community.

The role of the pastor

The pastor is the key in leading a congregation to build quality relationships to become an authentic, believing community. The pastor must maintain a close relationship with God in his or her devotional life and earnestly pray for deep and affectionate brotherly love in the Church. I try to give major time periods to prayer and fasting for unity and caring for one another in Faith Baptist Church. All true fellowship is accomplished by the Holy Spirit. Significantly, it is the Spirit which binds us with cords that cannot be broken.

The pastor must also set an example by showing real interest in the church members and love them unconditionally. We are all often influenced by others. I frequently say from tan he pulpit to the church, 'I love you and it's a joy being your pastor.' It is important for the pastor to be gentle, forgiving and patient, and develop a compassionate ministry and outreach to the sick. She or he must be willing to visit in homes and assist hurting and needy people when required. Caring for people's real needs will have to be the highest priority in order to succeed in creating a community.

I preach brotherly love and constantly encourage people to build quality relationships in the church by having a right attitude of heart towards one another. The Bible gives high priority to loving one another as the Lord commanded. As the Word is preached and taught, the Holy Spirit will apply the truth.

Lastly, the pastor must be focused in order to achieve the goal of creating a biblical community. The pastor will not be free from problems, because she or he is dealing with imperfect people. A considerable portion of my time has been used for problem-solving. It is very important for a pastor to be willing to face obstacles within the church which prevent real friendship and fellowship taking place. She or he must be pragmatic and learn to recognize a problem in its early stages before it gets out of hand. Once the problem is recognized one should not postpone tackling it, unpleasant as the thought may be. The pastor needs to develop the three vital skills of understanding human behaviour, predicting behaviour and influencing behaviour.

The contribution of the church members

The church members must be made aware that God is concerned about right relationships in the Church. It is the Lord's purpose to form each congregation into a united, harmonious family, exhibiting forbearance and mutual forgiveness for the world to see. We have the responsibility to co-operate with God to bring this into fruition.

The congregation must be equipped to build and maintain healthy relationships. Basic elements or factors of relationship such as trust, respect, love and understanding must be taught. Every year in Faith Baptist Church, one month is set aside to deal with issues of relationships.

Church members must be helped to connect and also encouraged to make effort to express affection and regard to each other, both in warm greetings and friendliness. The members must be approachable and cultivate unselfish, outgoing interest and support for one another. We establish community as we extend God's love to each other.

It is so important that the church assembles regularly for prayer because praying together creates a loving atmosphere. We must also engage in regular intercession for our fellow believers – for their spiritual and physical blessing. In our weekly church's prayer meetings and all-night prayer meetings people are prayed for. Here people's imperfections and flaws are not held against them. In real community you are encouraged to believe that with God's power you can overcome and transcend your limitations.

Regularly eating together and recreation also help create a community. The men in our church meet quarterly to play games and eat together; this has fostered closeness among them.

The formation of primary groups

The establishment of primary groups in the church helps create a sense of community. A primary group is small enough for everyone to be acquainted on a face-to-face first-name basis. In Faith Baptist Church, our primary groups provide a variety of opportunities for people to build relationships and have meaningful interactions. Individuals find personal significance and a sense of belonging in the primary groups. All the various primary groups have also provided more places and possibilities to assimilate people into the body.

We have Sunday school classes which meet weekly for about 45 minutes and Bible studies before the worship service. There is also a youth group (for 12–17-year-olds) and a young adults club (for 18–22-year-olds). We also have a choir and another musical group that sings contemporary Christian songs. In addition we have special interest groups such as Men's Fellowship and Women's Fellowship which meet regularly to deal with issues of interest.

Lastly, we have house groups. The purpose of the house group is for edification and building up one another. Our house groups are neither Bible study groups nor prayer groups. They exist to help members to grow together in Christ.

Those present at our midweek house groups are encouraged to share their struggles, doubts and burdens. A group of people hiding from one another will never experience edification. The members of the house groups serve as the instruments of grace for one another. They pray and minister to one another.

Local Church Leadership in Urban Communities

Jim Hart

Director of INCIT, a small project based in Liverpool.
Here he describes its experiment called 'Theology in the Community'

The problem

A manual worker who hears the call to professional ministry is compelled to become an academic. He may have been leading people into Christian faith for decades. He may be an autodidact, self-taught in Dickens and Byron, the Bible and Marx.[1] He may be an imaginative presenter of the gospel. No matter: to be a 'professional good man' he must set all this aside and steep himself in Christology, theories of salvation, missiology and church history. Churches of all denominations end up turning local leaders into 'puppets' who will conserve the old ways rather than 'prophets' who might lead God's people to new expressions of faith and witness.

Churches too mostly want the good old days to return when, as they nostalgically recall, their pews were full and they were the social centre of community life. That life is now disappearing under the attack of rampant consumerism; the church buildings decay and its leaders await the latest government initiative – 'SRB', Sure Start or whatever to give themselves something to do.

What is the Church for?

Our response to this analysis is called 'Theology in the Community'. This tries to understand and discard the giant weight of millennia of 'imperial', top-down religion. The edifice is collapsing and we can now dig out an authentic, primitive, simple Christian practice from beneath the ruins. It is a time of hope, not despair. We begin by saying: 'The sole purpose of the Church is to negotiate the Word of God', not to run activities or buildings. We then say: 'The Word must engage with the world, the text with the context.' It is where the eternal Word engages with the transient context – in time and place – in which the disclosure of God takes place. Armed with these two principles, God's people are freed from the treadmill of fund-raising, activities and committees to encounter him and invite their neighbours to join them in a journey of learning – 'growing in world and Word'.

Growing in world

We go out in circles: from me to my family, community, town, country, world and universe. We go from what we know to what we do not know; from here to there; and from now to then. This is a method, not a course, so we are not bound by a syllabus, do not have to pass an exam, or get a certificate. Here are some examples:

A teacher invites teenage children to a weekend to study the lives of some children of the world – small boys with Kalashnikovs in Aceh, armless children in Sierra Leone, and Elain Gonsales floating in the sea on an inner tube. We describe the geopolitical contexts and the children pore over maps. They end by making a statement about the rights of children and staging a play in a local drama festival. Their awareness has been enhanced for life.

Christian leaders, immersed in the constant struggles for good and affordable social housing, study *A Century of Public Housing*. This historical review shows them where they have come from and lessons they can apply to their present campaigns.

Local residents meet in one of their homes for a songs workshop. Each person plays a favourite song and tells why he or she likes it. We move from what they know (mostly popular broadcast songs) to what they do not know (work and political songs, ballads, lieder and cantata).

Groups have worked with me on all kinds of topics: Disney World and global tourism, war, the Irish conflict, Yugoslavia, Transcaucasia, Wal-Mart and football. We always start with the known, simplified media wisdom and end up in amazement at the complexities of each topic. People equip themselves to contest 'received wisdom'.

Growing in Word

Some people were reading the story of Jesus and Zacchaeus and a woman was reminded of the time when her son fell out of a tree. Later on she said: 'I like Jesus but I don't like God!' The leader commented later that she began with a family incident and ended up with Christology. You might ask what sessions on war and Disney World have got to do with Christianity. We can resort to a God confined in liturgy and shrine to escape from a bewildering modernity or seek him in it and be enabled to cope and flourish. We must release the Bible, our basic text, from tradition and prejudice if its ever-fresh, radical commentary on humanity is to be revealed. Here are some examples.

A church weekend includes *The City that God Wants*, a sequence of Scripture, song and poetry to contrast the two great symbolic cities, Babylon (the city as it is), and the new Jerusalem – the city that God wants. The oppression of Babylon is depicted with songs about mills, mines and seafarers.

The congregation on Sunday morning gets to the creed. Instead of saying it, they sit silently while a setting by Vivaldi is played. They are asked to meditate on its meaning. Vivaldi poignantly sets *Et incarnatus est* and *Crucifixus* and then bursts joyfully into *Et resurrexit*.[2] They encounter an over-familiar liturgy in a new way.

I decided years ago that I was looking for the 'Sermon on the Mount' church. I would adopt a minimalist creed of 'walking in the way of Jesus' and sit lightly to Christology, doctrines of the atonement, sacrament, baptism and so forth. We 'ordinary' people, it seemed to me, could walk in this Way and it would inspire us to oppose those who steal and misuse our commonwealth as well as enable us to cope with what they make us endure. We unlock the Bible in our own way. A friend says: 'It's not that the Bible is difficult. Much of it is straightforward. The difficulty is that we don't obey it.' This is the spirit of 'Theology in the Community'.

Notes

1 See *The Intellectual Life of the British Working Classes* (Jonathan Rose/ Yale Nota Bene, 2002).
2 They are given the Latin and English words.

New Models of Church

Stuart Murray Williams

Trainer and Consultant working under the auspices of the
Anabaptist network

Some talk about 'new ways of being Church' or 'emerging Church';
others wonder about 'future Church' or 'post-Church' groups. Some
enthuse about 'cell Church' or 'alternative worship' as authentic
forms of Christian community in a postmodern and post-Christen-
dom culture. Others are inspired by Jesus' table fellowship and
advocate 'Church around the table' as a place of encounter, intimacy
and real friendship. Some eschew neighbourhood models and plant
into the networks and subcultures that criss-cross our cities. Others
plead for incarnational Church among those who are marginal and
have no networks. The Church in the city – for this is where most
new models of Church are being pioneered – is becoming increasingly pluriform.

Much of this is experimental, tentative, exploratory, small-scale
and subversive. Some models are inspired by a search for authentic
community, others by a longing for less banal or programmatic
worship, others again by a passion for earthed and contextual
mission. Those involved can be single-minded, driven, desperate,
energetic, laid back, flexible, diffident, unassuming or any combination of these. Some are evangelicals and charismatics; others are
post-evangelicals and post-charismatics. Some draw on Celtic,
Orthodox or monastic spirituality, often eclectically; others are ener-
gized by the Anabaptist tradition or liberation theology. Whatever is
happening, it is messy and fluid, defying categorization but posing
important questions.

Underlying theological questions surface from time to time.
Should church be large or small, monocultural or multi-ethnic,
rooted in neighbourhoods or constructed along network lines, culturally attuned or counter-cultural? What does it mean to belong,
and how does belonging relate to believing and behaving? Should
we plant churches or work for the renewal of existing churches?
What is church anyway? What are the non-negotiables, and what
could be done differently? In fact, what is the gospel and where does
it connect with urban society? What does it mean to follow Jesus
and seek first his kingdom of justice and peace in the city?

What has inspired this creative chaos and provoked such questions? The interweaving of modernity and postmodernity, the end of Christendom and the repositioning of the Church on the social margins, the continuing decline of the churches and the prospect of meltdown within 30 years, the disappearance of 1,500 people from the churches each week, the minimal impact of most evangelistic strategies, deeper engagement with local communities and sub-cultures. The jury may be out on these new models of church for some time yet, but the questions are significant and the experimentation is vital. The urban Church is passing through the pain and joys of rebirth.

Urban Expression is a network of small Christian communities taking root in east London, bound together not by denominational loyalty or a common strategy but by shared and deeply held values. In six local communities, small groups of Christians are asking what it means to incarnate the good news and to live out the Jesus story. In one community this means restoring a neglected playground and developing a bike project for joy-riders. In another it means establishing a friendship centre where members of different ethnic groups can build trust and relationships. For some it means learning Sylhetti; for others it means using drama to teach non-violence in schools; for others again it means opening homes to those with mental illness.

The aim is clear – to plant churches in these communities and to encourage people to discover the good news of Jesus. But the approach is patient and subversive, so that what emerges is incarnational, from the grass roots, not imposed from outside. One group waited for the local community to name the church that was developing; they also avoided the loaded terms 'Church' and 'Christians' and used 'followers of Jesus' to describe themselves. Measured against church growth or suburban church-planting standards, these initiatives are slow and unimpressive. They are small, vulnerable and have yet to demonstrate that they can thrive or even survive. Urban Expression is not a success story but it may eventually result in new models of church coming to birth.[1]

What does Urban Expression represent?

- Partnerships rooted in shared values rather than doctrinal agreement, fixed patterns or institutional relationships.

- Perseverance year after year, sensitivity to the Spirit rather than being driven by goals, and long-term investment in local communities.
- Willingness to be creative, to ask no-holds-barred questions about Church and mission, to take risks.
- Openness about financial needs and rediscovery of *koinonia* as economic as well as spiritual community.
- Freedom to experiment coupled with accountability and mutual support.
- A conviction that the gospel of the kingdom of God really is good news in the city, but only as it is lived out in the community.

Urban Expression is one example of the gradual emergence of new models of church and new approaches to mission in the cities. There are many others. Not all will thrive or make lasting contributions to the cities, although even the 'failures' will offer clues and resources for future developments. Nor will they quickly replace inherited forms of church that have served the cities faithfully for generations. The inherited Church and the emerging Church need each other; partnership and mutual respect will enable both to learn from each other. Valuing tradition and welcoming new ideas, drawing on experience and allowing fresh approaches to challenge assumptions: the cities need churches that are humble, open, secure enough to listen and not to cling desperately to fixed old patterns or inflexible new models, aware that ethos is more significant than structure and attitudes more important than attributes.

Note

1 For more information about Urban Expression, visit www.urbanexpression.org.uk or contact Urban Expression, PO Box 35238, London E1 4YA. See also p. 137.

Questions for Further Thought and Action

1 Find out the story of your local church. How did it begin? What phases has it been through? What is its current mission?

2 What enables relationships within your church to grow? Work at this. What damages relationships? Guard against this.

3 What are the characteristics of a 'city that God wants'? Design your ideal city. How can your church help this to become a reality?

4 What ways of doing and being Church might connect with different groups of people in your locality? Ask some of them to help you work on this.

3

Spirituality and Worship

This chapter examines what is perhaps the most distinctive thing which Christians do in the city – worship the one Triune God. This is our calling as believers, to render him all honour and praise. But how do we do that in an environment which dishonours and disrespects the Creator by disfiguring and degrading his creation?

Our contributors look at the problems and the possibilities of urban spirituality, at both the personal and the corporate level. They give clues as to how we can incorporate our urban experience into our God-life. This includes both positive and negative – art and relationships as well as poverty and racism.

The approaches tread the fine line between the immanent and the transcendent: encouraging us to bring in our experience of dislocation as well as helping us to rise above it, living on the victory side.

Chris Burch gives a personal account of how spiritual practice can help us avoid burnout, without reducing prayer to a psychological tool, resorting to the platitudes of New Age nostrums, or following the escapism of pietistic Christianity.

Pete Hobson has written a deep, touching account of his wrestling with the question of how to lead worship authentically amid the pain of his inner-city congregations. The ineffability of God connects here with the ineffability of the urban.

Jacqueline Brown contributes a flavour of the explosion in Pentecostal worship in our inner cities. She articulates and illustrates the way in which exuberant praise both energizes and empowers believers in inner-city congregations for mission and for life.

Doug Gay shows us some of the ways in which creativity and the arts can be used to renew urban worship. He demonstrates that the arts are as relevant to tired traditional churches as to youthful 'alternative' congregations.

Maintaining Hope: How to Keep Going and Not Burn Out

Chris Burch

Formerly Vicar of St Agnes', Burmantofts in inner-city Leeds, and Precentor of Coventry Cathedral. He is now priest-in-charge of St Peter's, Braunstone Park, an outer council estate in Leicester

I'm not an expert on burnout. But I do know what its early stages feel like. You could say it's my fault for getting involved – but who ministers in Urban Priority Areas (UPAs) while remaining calm and detached? I've taken risks and made mistakes – I've gone out on a limb and seen it being sawn off or, worse still, have realized I'm sawing it off myself! At the same time I'm committed to the God who changes lives and answers prayer. I've got involved, and I've been splatted by my own weaknesses and the gritty realities of the communities and people I'm called to serve. By middle age some of my minister colleagues have burned out. Others are cynics – they have taken the armour-plated option to avoid the pain. Do I have to go the same way? Here are a few ideas for those who want to answer 'No.'

You are not alone

Almost every sign of UPA ministry stress – tiredness, hurt, frustration, confusion, above all, anger – is made worse when we are, or feel, isolated. Yet we belong to the Body of Christ, the fellowship of Jesus' people across the world and down history. We need our brothers and sisters for support. Who are our allies? And if we can't see who they are, how can we find them?

Finding support from within the congregation

Some ministers don't feel they can get close to members of their own churches. But why? When Paul was left for dead in Lystra, it was the believers (his converts) who gathered round him and put him together again (Acts 14.20). My ministry in Leeds began in confusion and weakness – it was the lay leaders who spent time with me and prayed with me, who set the course for ministry later.

Finding support from the institutional Church

Often the rest of the Church doesn't quite know what to make of ministry in UPAs, especially if it includes risk-taking. But someone in the renewal movement once said, 'If you want your leaders to trust you, then trust them. Tell them what you are doing – and ask for their blessing.' I felt so vulnerable at one stage in Leeds that I rang the bishop to tell him what we were doing, so that he wouldn't hear from the *News of the World* (it didn't get to that point – but I didn't know that at the time). He was very supportive and encouraging. Now, in my new parish, I couldn't wish for better support from my bishop and archdeacon.

Finding support from praying communities and resource people

When at my beam-ends, I've asked for prayer from a religious community. I've been helped to grow by groups like the Community of Celebration (Fisherfolk), the Anglican Benedictines at Burford Priory, and a Christian Growth and Gestalt Therapy group. I go regularly to see a wise spiritual counsellor and share my spiritual ups and downs with her. Find someone to whom you can tell *anything* – then you don't have to be polite or put on your religious mask with them.

Take it to the Lord in prayer

No Christian finds prayer easy, but for many of us it is made harder by guilt that we cannot soar effortlessly to the heavenly places. The Christian life is a *walk* with God, not a soaring flight, and plodding along in prayer is normal. When we are in difficulties, it can feel like walking through porridge. Sometimes, it feels impossible. That's when a companion in prayer can make the difference between keeping going and giving up. Here are some other ideas, tried and tested by others – I have found them helpful too.

Be real with your feelings

I have sat through Morning Prayer and admitted at the end, 'God, that was a complete waste of time . . .' It wasn't – God never wastes time spent with him – but that's how it felt. I have nothing to prove to God, so if I'm a complete failure as a minister (which I'm not, but it sometimes feels like that too) I'm still OK with him. Sometimes feelings can be turned into prayers. 'God, I'm tired!' – just a shallow blasphemy, or a prayerful breathing out from the depth of my soul at the end of a bruising day? 'God, that's appalling!' – if we have any of God's Spirit within us, God shares our anger and hurt at the injustice and pain we see all around us. And the idea can be stretched into wonder too: 'Oh God, that's beautiful!'

Creative use of Scripture
The Bible is full of resources to catch our imaginations and spirits and point them towards God. For instance, Jesus used the Psalms, and his followers have prayed them ever since. Some of them could have been written for UPA ministers living on the edge – look at Psalm 69. One reason for a prayer routine that is set for us – based on Psalms, Scripture readings and Scripture-based prayers – is that it does not depend on our efforts or gifts, but sets God's story along-side ours. 'Didn't our hearts burn within us, as he walked with us and taught us from the Scriptures?' What would it be like to pray through Psalm 69, phrase by phrase, on behalf of the world's poor, or the people of my council estate parish?

Praying through stories
A community is defined by its shared stories, and one way of getting in touch with fellow members of Christ's Body is by praying into their stories. This can be done using our imaginations and even our senses – for instance, if I am praying into the story in Mark 2.1–12, I can ask, 'What do I see? What do I hear? feel? smell? taste?' Then, as the action unfolds, 'What is going on?' And, at the end, 'What are the main characters saying to me? – to each other? What do I want to say to them?' This method can be used on Bible stories, on our own stories, or on stories of the world's poor. It is a way of using magazines like the *New Internationalist* that avoids the guilt-trap I feel when reading about people I ought to help but can't. In this way I can at least stand with them in prayer.[1]

These are only a few ideas for pilgrims along the tougher stretches of the Christian road. For further reading – well, I browse in second-hand theological bookshops or ask friends and mentors.

Note

1 The classic Ignatian method of prayer is introduced in Gerard Hughes' *God of Surprises* (Darton, Longman & Todd, 1985). But my favourite book on it is *Praying the Kingdom*, by Charles Elliott (Darton, Longman & Todd, 1985).

Worship: Making it Real in the City?

Pete Hobson

Vicar, Church of the Martyrs, Leicester – a lively church, set at the diverse city-centre edge of a multiracial, multifaith city

There are some places, or perhaps some temperaments, or perhaps the right combination of the two, where worship in church is in itself a good experience. The music, the words, the setting, all combine to produce a result not only aesthetically pleasing but spiritually uplifting. Sadly, for me this has seldom been the case. I suspect it is in part due to temperament, but to a larger degree due to the settings in which I have ministered – which have always been urban, and for the most part exceedingly inner-city urban. In such places, and in my experience, as both a worship leader and participant, the important question is not 'How good is this?' but 'How real?'

The thesis of this piece is that the job of worship, at least in an urban setting, is to bring reality into our thinking and living – in short, to 'make it real'.

I'm immediately conscious of a counter-argument. For some people, especially in urban places, the nature of their living is such that what they are looking for in worship is something different, a temporary escape from the painful reality that is their life. I don't deny that is the motive of some in coming to church. I do dispute that the proper function of the Church is to collude with that, at least in the long term. If, by doing the other things that I will be outlining, some counter-point to the painful realities of life is discerned, then so much the better. But for me worship is not about escapism, but about engaging with and ultimately defeating the powers that claim to shape our lives.

So what would 'make it real' look like in an urban setting? The best I can do is to attempt to describe the principles I've brought to attempting that task in four different places, over 26 years – in Brunswick and then Old Trafford, in Manchester in the late 1970s and 1980s; in Hackney in the 1990s, and now in Leicester.

We should begin with the real lives people live. Of course, there are well-adjusted, happy and fulfilled people living in inner cities. And of course misery can be found anywhere. But as generalizations go, it is as true as any to say that inner-city lives have more than their share of misery. The city is disproportionately full of people damaged by life, but seeking meaning or perhaps just pain relief, in church and in its worship. How do I, as worship planner and leader, aim to respond? By ensuring that what I do offers as much opportunity as I can to engage with the realities that are their lives, while giving every opportunity for them to choose how far, if at all, they take up that opportunity on any given occasion. To seek to challenge the oppressive forces in someone's life by the coercive oppression of a worship leader would be truly and ironically abusive. Sadly, that can happen!

I believe in doing this 'real engagement' from three perspectives. First, we need to seek to be real in what we say and do, and in what we ask others to say and do. This is human reality, as opposed to game-playing. Second, we need to seek the reality of the living God that lies behind and beyond all the words we use. This is spiritual reality as opposed to spiritual absence. Third, we need to see the reality that means that what we do in church makes a difference to lives outside church. This is community reality, as opposed to irrelevance.

How do we do these things? Too much of our worship is mere word games. Now I recognize that a certain amount of game-playing can be healthy, or at least harmless. But what is worship for? Surely it is about making the connections between our lives and God's purposes for us and his world. And to do this, we need to be prepared to be real in what we say and do. No liturgy, whether formal or informal, can ensure this. But plenty of liturgies, of either kind, can protect us from it. Two things I have found helpful in this respect: the first is (sometimes) to pause in introducing prayer or song and invite people to reflect on the words, and not to use them unless they are sure they want to. The second is to introduce pauses in the flow of worship in order to invite people to reflect on what they are thinking about 'right now' – and maybe to talk to a neighbour about it, if they dare! How we use such opportunities is up to us. But if we never even have them, how can we use them at all?

The reality of God in worship is even harder to plan for. People find it in so many different ways, and what is working for me one day may be doing the opposite for you at the very same time. But again, it is a journey we might agree we are mutually embarked upon.

Reality within our community is perhaps easier to comprehend, even if equally challenging to ensure. One test of it might be to check mentally all the elements of a particular service afterwards (or, if you're brave, as you go along) to see what there is which is in any way affected by or hoping to affect the life of the person who lives opposite your church but never comes into it. And saying that you are praying for him or her doesn't count!

How to sum up what I'm trying to say? There's a song which in itself is perhaps no better, no worse than many of its kind: short, with a simple melody, and words which express a devotional intent that can be either helpful or not, depending on many factors. But of this particular song I have some very strong memories.

One is of it being sung as a solo in one church where I worked, by a woman I'll call Sarah, whose life experience had taught her that if she was to find any strength or safety, it was what she carved out for herself, and whose church experiences had not been exactly easy. But in this church Sarah *had* found something different, and that night she sang this song with all her heart, as if it had been written solely for her.

The other memory is of a prayer meeting at my current church, singing the same song. And next to me was a middle-aged man, Andy, and he was singing along, with his whole heart, soul and mind, and as loud as anyone there. But he didn't sing the words: he has Down's Syndrome. He never fails to come to our services – usually late. He knows where he belongs, and he knows that to sing his heart out is acceptable here. That is what making it real in the city means to me. The song?

> God of Grace – I turn my face to you, I cannot hide . . .
> . . . and your grace clothes me in righteousness . . .
> . . . I stand complete in you.[1]

Note

1 From *New Mission Praise* (Marshall Pickering, 1996). 'God of Grace' © copyright 1990 Sovereign/Lifestyle Music. Used by permission. sovereignmusic@aol.com

Urban Worship

Jacqueline Brown

Pastor, Lighthouse Community Church, Ladbroke Grove, London; and
Director, Inspire Schools Ministry

My perspective of worship is in the locality of Ladbroke Grove, London. Worship is 'poetic', and very 'raw' in its expression: an uninhibited expression of exuberation; a liberating metamorphosis of our response towards the overwhelming kindness and goodness of God.

When I was first asked to make a contribution to this book, my initial thoughts were that urban worship is R 'n' B, Garage, Hip-Hop. I wanted to focus on the type of sound that comes from what the local/national Christian press calls urban praise and worship. As I spoke with musicians who were worship leaders, they all seemed to equate urban worship with the soulful grooves that come from black music. In my quest to get to the root of the overall definition I have discovered that urban worship is much more than mere music and singing, and to reduce worship to this kind of thinking would be a tragedy.

Twenty-first-century worship is much more than tradition: it has become more emotive. Certainly from a Pentecostal perspective, people want to feel the experience of worship. They want to touch God spiritually, physically, psychologically and emotionally. Coming from a city church context, urban worship in our city is culturally expressive, dynamic and relevant to the generation we seek to lead into praise and worship.

The word 'urban' embraces inner-city culture, which is unique to inner cities. London has a culture unique to itself but within that culture there are many sub-cultures. The word 'worship' expresses paying homage to someone or something as deity. Putting 'urban' and 'worship' together could be described in this way: 'An outward expression of God culturally of an inner transformation of self uniquely.'

There is a desperate desire to relinquish what is perceived as 'old, outdated' tradition, almost at the expense of not realizing that traditions are a fact of life. Just when we think we have rid ourselves of them, we have already formed new ones.

When you read the Christian press and visit Christian book and music outlets, urban worship is linked to music and singing, with musical styles primarily by black American artists such as Ron Kenoly, Alvin Slater and Donnie McClurkin.

It seems that what really dictates urban worship is dependent on which city you are from, the class structure of that society and the culture of that city. One such example is the city of Manchester where there is a famous band called The Tribe. This group leads worship from a sub-culture unique to their inner-city environment. They lead the youth into raising their hands, jumping and dancing and speaking out words which are almost like poetry with a drum-beat to it. In London you have Watchman who leads worship Hip-Hop style but more 'Ragga', which is a type of reggae.

The Lighthouse Community Fellowship (LCF), a satellite of Kensington Temple, has had the privilege of being part of a city church yet engaging in urban worship. Our worship is 'Street', incorporating all styles of music, with the exception possibly of Hip-Hop, although we have merged youth and adult worship as an experiment. While organically growing over the last four years we have learnt many things.

Learning curve

For respondents who cannot sing or play an instrument well yet have a heart for worship, it is preferable not to enlist them as part of the worship team: it is better if you put them in a choir. I hear you ask, 'Why?' We tried this and it nearly split the church, let alone our worship team. If someone just does not have the ability to sing or play, they just don't!

For respondents who are extremely talented but have not dealt with the issue of pride, do not put them on the worship team (we tried this with a very talented musician who subsequently let us down when we were called up for a major project. When challenged, eventually the person joined another group where they could get more prestige).

Ascertain at the beginning whether they are an artist, a performer, an entertainer or a worshipper. Unhoned performers draw people to themselves; worshippers draw people to God.

Insist that the team makes worship a lifestyle, not an event. This will enhance the team's efforts and sensitivity to the Holy Spirit.

Without it the services will be stale, staid and dry. The team has developed a 12-week learning programme to train worshippers in the area of worship.

Human ideas in worship can lead to catastrophe in a church service or at any worship event. Be sensitive. Enquire from God what to do. I am reminded of David in the Bible when he thought it was a good idea to carry the ark of the Presence of God on a new cart; when it stumbled, one of the men tried to steady it, which led to death (1 Chronicles 13; 2 Samuel 6).

What is urban worship?

Urban worship brings people into the presence of Jesus. We seek for people to encounter God every time we come into a place of praise and worship. Here are a few tips that we have learnt at Lighthouse Community Fellowship about leading people into urban praise and worship.

- *Start as you mean to go on.* Always remember when you start to worship you are not rehearsing, you are worshipping, so always do it with all your heart and in truth. Be sensitive.
- *Be discerning.* Although you will have almost always prepared a list of songs to do, during your worship time pray for wisdom and listen to the Holy Spirit.
- *Be clear* and let the congregation know what you require them to do.
- *Be engaging and interactive* when the moment necessitates this.
- *Know when to pull the music back.* Keep people focused on God. Do not allow the music to take over the worship. Enhance the worship by being a conduit for the Holy Spirit to flow through you to the people, so they will participate fully in worship. Remember: skill plus the Holy Spirit equals excellence.

There is so much more which could be said about how to lead worship. However, as we learn and grow, our best course of action is to be sensitive to the Holy Spirit. Develop your practical ability: this facilitates worship. Pray. Be theologically sound in doctrine. Trust that God will use each person in the team, i.e. musicians, worship singers and worship leader, to lead people into experiencing the presence of a Holy God in the beauty of his holiness.

Worship Alternatives:
Use of Arts and Creativity in Worship

Doug Gay

Formerly Pastor of Clapton United Reformed Church in Hackney,
east London, and now doing a PhD on preaching in Glasgow

I first shared in the worship of an urban congregation in Hackney, east London, at Rectory Road URC in 1984. The church had 25 members, a new Scottish minister and a congregation of 50 per cent white, 25 per cent African-Caribbean, and 25 per cent African.

Those of us working to plan services soon found ourselves in a common dilemma. We wanted the worship to be family friendly, but felt that family services often short-change both children and adults. The solution we worked out involved starting church at 10.30 a.m. for adults with children and anyone else who wanted to come. Adults had an adult Sunday School. After gathering in one group for singing and telling the story, kids went to an age-related group to work on an activity. This overlapped the service start time of 11 a.m., and the opening part of the church service was led by a 'lay' church member. At 11.15, we came together in church. Now instead of a 'kids' talk', the *kids talked*, and danced, rapped, sang, showed pictures – ministering *to* the whole church. At 11.30, the kids went out while the adults had a sermon. After intercessions, or before Communion, kids returned for the end of the service.

We used Scripture Union's *Learning Together* material, with a Bible base for every week (although, frustratingly, not lectionary based). A group met mid-week to read the passage, reflect on it and plan activities. We aimed to create and develop new resources each week – songs and sketches were written and an approach to the passage shared across the groups and developed in the sermon. Work with children became a centre for creativity, at the heart of our worshipping life (maybe too much so?) and children were both ministered to and ministers.

Working with a multicultural team – Scottish, Jamaican, Irish, Ghanaian, Welsh, 'Black British', English (black and white)[1] – led to introducing styles and forms from across those cultures. Folk melodies from various countries, rap and reggae styles, songs in different mother tongues, songs from different religious traditions –

our diversity enlarged our worship vocabulary, within an ethos of affirming and celebrating the whole range of cultures represented there.

I returned in 1988 to the Greater Easterhouse area of Glasgow and settled in the housing estate of Ruchazie. The worship culture of the, at first entirely white, Scottish church, was more traditional, but work with children drew on much of the material from Hackney, sometimes recontextualized in Scots/Glasgow vernacular. The worship resources produced by Scripture Union and others made some attempt to be responsive to multicultural Britain, but life in an outer-city estate was rarely pictured in material mostly dominated by suburban images.

From 1989, I became involved in the Late, Late Service (LLS) – an 'alternative' worship service inspired by Sheffield's Nine O'Clock Service (NOS). Their worship was influenced by the growth of club culture, where 'raves' were being held in increasingly sophisticated visual environments. LLS followed them in a radical remoulding of the worship space, creating a space in the round, where projected images – slides and video – created ambience, to explore ideas and respond to scriptural themes and passages. The turn to the body, seen in the use of dance music, was also evident in the eclectic use of ritual. A major dimension was the visual refurbishment of liturgy to connect with contemporary urban culture, global and local. This connection was meant to celebrate and to offer a prophetic challenge to late twentieth-century culture.[2] Images from NASA of the earth from space were set alongside images of Glasgow we made ourselves. The ambience of a service ranged from still and meditative to loud, harsh and energetic.

The services reflected the angst and confusion of the fiercely democratic group who planned and prepared them; men dominated some of the technology, but planning and leadership were shared tasks. Enormously hungry for time and energy, frustratingly erratic in quality, viewed as a curiosity by the wider church in Glasgow, given almost no financial help from the mainstream Church, and damaged by the fallout from the NOS scandal, LLS held together a stable core which grew from five to 50 in five years and whose influence was felt nationally and internationally.

In 1995 I returned to Hackney to become minister of a tiny URC in Clapton, fronting the road known as 'Murder Mile'. The church was small, elderly, mostly white and definitely run by the white members. Its worship culture reflected a traditional Congregational model, with little acknowledgement of cultural diversity.

The task I agreed with the elders was to evolve morning worship into a family-friendly format while planting a new 'alternative' congregation in the evening. Both services began very small – there were no children in the church, so it was 'Field of Dreams' – *if we build it they will come*; the evening began with six of us meeting and sharing dreams and visions for reshaping Church in the city.

A crucial issue in the life of the church was to shift the range of cultures which were being endorsed and displayed in worship. We drew on the US African-American hymnal *Lead Me, Guide Me*, and on the Iona Community songbooks. African members taught us songs from their countries. The way the church fellowshipped and ate together became a celebration of our diversity. After three years, the elders and I felt able to plan a church weekend, which was a crucial moment in building community – using story-telling, art workshops for young and old, and video.

The evening congregation also grew, though there was a divide between those who were more 'hardcore' about the quality of the media/artforms and engagement with wider London culture, and those who were more focused on their relationships to the local community.

We faced the 'family service' dilemma again, with attendances ranging from 40 to 70 and many under-fives in the congregation. Despite worries from older members, our monthly family service moved into a circle gathered around a centrepiece relevant to our theme. After singing together and story-telling the Scripture, we evolved a time called Exploring the Word, when people moved to tables or groups of chairs placed around the corners of the room and worked on paintings, collage, sketches and conversations about the passage. Young and old worked together, with one group aimed at the youngest and another at the most reluctant joiners-in. After 15 minutes, a song brought people together, to show each group's work, share prayers of joy and concern, and close our 50-minute service. The format threatened people's sense of appropriate behaviour in church; some older people found it difficult, but mostly it worked.

Looking back over 20 years, I am conscious of God at work creating community in these different settings, where communities have been encouraged to be creative. The static, linear, wordy worship, which has been revised, embodied a set of assumptions about class, culture and gender at odds with postmodern living, and diminished the creativity of God's grace to us in the Incarnation. The Spirit in the city calls us to worship – worship for bodies and souls, worship that celebrates and explores the diversity of the world, worship that feeds the soul through the senses, worship that treasures the involvement of all ages, worship that is always shaped by political realities locally and globally, worship that puts pictures to the words – worship that fits us for the city to come, where beauty and truth will be reunited, where we will be free at last for godly play.

Notes

1 This is how different team members described themselves.
2 The example of Adbusters and their work of subvertising was important: www.adbusters.com

---

Questions for Further Thought and Action

1 (a) What causes some Christian people to give up and drop out of urban congregations? Find out the stories of any known to you.
   (b) How could things be different? What has helped you to maintain hope?

2 What are the realities in your locality which need to be incorporated into your congregational worship? How could you do that?

3 (a) How can the various idioms and forms of human expression in music, words, visual and performing arts in your community be drawn upon in developing styles of worship in your neighbourhood?
   (b) Where is the Spirit blowing? Where is the Life that you can tap into for your congregational worship?

4 Explore ways of involving the whole congregation in developing inclusive and participatory worship experiences.

4

Scripture

Christians are known as people of the book, but it is the book – or at least the form of the book, literary, wordy – that causes barriers for so many people in our increasingly non-book culture, both among can-read-but-don't-read people on estates as well as the intellectual postmoderns.

In addition, the concerns of traditional readings of Scripture – purity, separation, individualism, religion – have less and less relevance for people not steeped in religious upbringings.

Finally, the wholly other-worldly projection of faith into a super-sensory world has led to the separation of faith from the mundane and everyday, as well as the political and social realities which shape and determine the existence of inner-city dwellers.

John Vincent supplies us with an understanding of a liberation-reading of Scripture. This hermeneutic 'from the underside' locates our Bible reading practice within the experiences of the poor and marginalized, and makes it easier for us to link Bible reading with political action with and alongside them.

Jenny Richardson shows us a method for relating Scripture to people's everyday experiences. This does not privilege the expert, but welcomes the diverse voices of the ordinary person. The approach helps them to see that their perspective has something to contribute in understanding the source book of their faith.

Roger Sainsbury rescues preaching from both conservative idolatry and radical neglect. Where the former elevate it into a shibboleth, urban practitioners too often dismiss its potential to deliver the Word of life. Roger shows how preaching can engage with urban social realities, and how such homiletics can build up the Church as a celebrational community within the wider neighbourhood.

Bible Study: The Liberation Theology Method

John Vincent
Emeritus Director of the Urban Theology Unit, Sheffield

The liberation theology method of working with the Bible has become the natural and favoured method for many urban church practitioners. The method itself can be described as a hermeneutic. The word 'hermeneutic' literally means 'meaning', but it is used to describe the process whereby meaning is worked out from the text, especially Scripture. Hermeneutic is, then, a method for getting from one thing to another, in two ways.

First, there is the process whereby we take a piece of passage or saying of Scripture, and seek to get meaning from it, or interpret it, in our own situation or experience. This is the journey from the text over into our context. By itself, it is often called the *deductive* method. We declare the text's meaning or value or message for us today by taking the text at its face value, and 'translating' it into our context today.

Second, there is the process whereby we take a piece of our own situation or context, or a piece of our experience, or community life, and seek to get perspectives for it, by taking it over into the world of Scripture. This is the journey from the context into the text. It can be called the *inductive* method. We find the experience's meaning by referring to pieces of Scripture in order to expand, elucidate or discover revelation in our experience.

Liberation theology always begins with the second. But it is not every kind of situation or experience that, for liberation theology, is seen as the appropriate starting point. The situation seen as most productive is that of oppression, and the experience seen as most productive is that of being victimized or oppressed.

From these vantage points (Action 1), we then discover that the biblical records are in fact precisely about people trying to make sense of, or experience God, in the midst of oppressive situations and in the face of oppressing people (Action 2). So we return to our own life and activity with learnings and solidarity, based on our encounters with the text (Action 3) (Figure 4.1).

We discover that the Scriptures emphasize precisely the things that people in situations of oppression, or undergoing personal

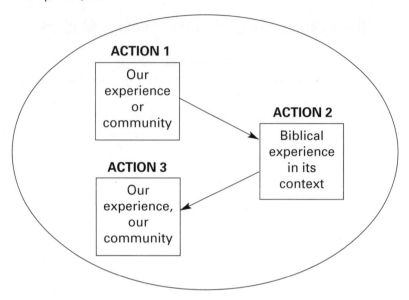

Figure 4.1: Liberation theology: hermeneutic method

oppression, need to hear as 'good news', and need to take into their lives as liberating practice, or action. The Boff brothers list such 'veins' in Scripture as:

> God the Father of life,
> God the Advocate of the oppressed,
> Liberation from the house of bondage,
> The prophecy of a new world,
> The Kingdom given to the poor,
> The church as total sharing.[1]

These are the questions which the poor have. But the poor seek life, life 'to the full' (John 10.10). The Boffs comment: 'This means that questions relevant to or urgent for the poor are bound up with the transcendental questions of conversion, grace, resurrection.'[2] The matters which we often think belong to interior, personal religion – conversion, grace and resurrection – are thus revealed as belonging to practical, everyday activity and real-life experience.

The Bible is thus seen in liberation theology as stressing:

Application rather than Explanation,
A Book of Life, not strange stories,
Transforming Energy within the texts,
Texts in their Social Contexts.[3]

The result of all this is not primarily wonderment, or piety, or spiritual devotion – though all are appropriate also. The result of it all is action, practice, commitment, conversion, change, politics, community building, and discovering the Kingdom of God on earth. The result may be in various specific actions, such as:

Confirmation of our own experiences as the poor,
Solidarity with oppressed people – Taking sides,
Setting up a project to create change,
Personal radical lifestyle moves –
    Downsizing, moving house, changing jobs.[4]

This liberating biblical hermeneutic is especially relevant to the urban Church. First, because people living in poor or oppressed situations and communities discover their 'brothers and sisters' in the text. There is a natural way in which urban people and urban Christians feel 'at home' in the biblical stories, especially those in the Gospels:

Occasionally, the simple, down-to-earth stories of the happenings in the days of Jesus actually get through, and you can understand the stories even if not the sermons supposedly designed to explain or 'preach on' them. Thus the inner city disciple occasionally hears of disciples being fishermen (Mark 1.16–20), being called provincial Galileans (Acts 2.7), unlearned and ignorant (Acts 4.13). Or they hear of people asking in astonishment where Jesus got his teachings from (Mark 6.2), and wonder what happened to that tradition in the contemporary educated Church.[5]

Further, the urban Christian finds a Jesus very much 'at home' in the urban scene today:

Here is Jesus, a small-town local hero, with working people around him, walking and acting and speaking to and about local people and places. The context could be anywhere where someone is street-wise, knows the local scene, loves the local folk, and retells local down-to-earth stories which confirm the attitudes and preconceptions of the culture. It is not the geographical context but the social and cultural context that gives sense to it all, and places the hero in the easily comprehensible role of local community spokesperson, catalyst and natural leader.[6]

The liberation theology urban experience of gospel realities is opening up a whole new way in which the Scriptures are being heard. The result is that a new biblical practice-theology is beginning to emerge, as the churches and people of the urban scene bring their discoveries and revelations so that all may learn from them.[7]

The invitation to a liberation theology way of using the Bible is thus beginning to bear fruit for the world and the wider Church. But its genius and its practice need to stay firmly in the contemporary academy of the gospel, the urban people themselves.

Notes

1 Leonardo Boff and Clodovis Boff, *Introducing Liberation Theology* (Burns & Oates, 1987, p. 32).
2 Boff and Boff, *Introducing Liberation Theology*, p. 33.
3 Boff and Boff, *Introducing Liberation Theology*, pp. 33–4.
4 Boff and Boff, *Introducing Liberation Theology*, pp. 33–4.
5 John Vincent, 'An Urban Hearing of the Gospel' in C. Rowland and J. Vincent (eds), *Gospel from the City* (Urban Theology Unit, 1977, pp. 105–16, p. 106).
6 Vincent, 'An Urban Hearing', p. 108.
7 See especially *Faithfulness in the City*, ed. John Vincent (St Deiniol's Library, 2003).

Unlocking Real Life!

Jenny Richardson

Church Army Staff Development Officer, Wilson Carlile College of
Evangelism. She was Chief Executive of Unlock (formerly the
Evangelical Urban Training Project) from 1993 to 2002

A new church member arrived at the home group: 'I'd like you to
pray. I've got a son who's slightly autistic, who's being bullied at
school . . . he doesn't have the designer wear . . . my sister-in-law
gets stuff from ram-raids, and can get a full kit for a fiver. Now I'm a
Christian, should I get the kit, or just carry on with the cheap stuff?
. . . but it's my son who's suffering, not me' . . . and the group now
had its study topic for the evening meeting!

Sue,[1] a team rector in an Urban Priority Area of East Hull,
described this 'Unlock style'[2] as 'honest, real, personal, experience
based . . . being who you are, and letting that speak', adding that
'Jesus taught by actions, with stories, with everyday things'. She had
felt inadequate alongside clergy from more academic backgrounds,
and described her first encounter with Unlock methods at a clergy
event: 'It just felt like coming home . . . I didn't know that I knew so
much . . . for me it was very much a confidence booster.' This
approach to theological learning[3] was for her and the Anglican
congregation where she had responsibility, and was shared with
other churches in the area. Sue co-ordinated a series of ecumenical
Bible study groups within the local community. I listened to the
experiences of those involved, and will share insights that emerged.

The method

Sue produced group materials, based on Unlock's method (Figure
4.2).[4] She used a picture of a wedding to begin to get people
talking,[5] and offered a Bible passage asking people to make connections, placing a Bible story alongside shared life experiences as a
gesture of solidarity. Sue offered the Bible story and questions on
one sheet, avoiding the need to handle a large book with overwhelming quantity of text.

Anna affirmed the method: 'Scripture passages linked to life experiences, sparked things in life . . . In the past, we've studied these
things but we don't see the link with everyday life.' Jackie had been

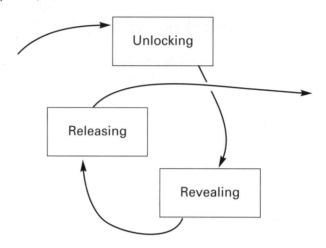

Figure 4.2: Unlock's method (© Unlock)

used to 'more formal Bible studies'; this was 'more user friendly . . . In our group, the majority of us had been going to church for donkeys' years, and done study on study . . . these brought out different things.'

Sheila laughed, 'We didn't find any difficulty with people talking, did we?! . . . it was stopping it! We did have one or two reserved people, but the others made up for it!'

Olivia saw this involvement as a consequence of 'material that's asking for people's experience. It starts people off and you can't stop them talking, which is good because in some groups people don't speak.'

Audrey expressed surprise at how much she knew; the process 'triggers something off', and Anna explained, 'We've got more to give than we ever realize when we start out.' Shirley recalled 'telling about things that you'd forgotten about: "Ooh, aye, I remember", but you haven't remembered for a long time. We thoroughly enjoyed it.'

Sue had worried that there was not enough material: 'They'll sit twiddling their thumbs', but Burmy's experience was that 'There was a bit too much. It took nearly half the session on the first question. We had to keep bringing them back to things. I found that we diversified so much.'

Group leaders

Sue identified and recruited group leaders: 'The main thing is they weren't to be clergy! It was people who people would have confidence in . . . but who didn't have so much knowledge that people would be intimidated . . . The other thing was friendliness . . . non-threatening, but good with people.'

Sheila, a potential leader, had been wary: 'I didn't know what to expect. I've always been too scared, too embarrassed.' Burmy echoed this, despite competence as a departmental sister in a hospital: 'It's a different field, and I'm an infant in the church, very shaky on lots of things . . . Leading a group that was well established in the church, and got their feet much more firmly than I have, I was hesitant.' Like leaders of other groups, they collaborated. 'We were able to help each other,' Sheila explained.

Sue facilitated a group leaders' training session: 'How Jesus taught . . . and asking people how they'd learned . . . We did the first week's study, based on weddings . . . people got so into the Bible study, they forgot that they were learning about doing one! . . . people quickly got to a very honest, personal level, talking about their own weddings, their own marriages . . . We looked back, to see what had been helpful, what had not been helpful, how to cope with different things . . . everybody said at the end, "Oh, if that's what it's like, then I feel more confident."' Sue also provided input on group work, encouraging people to link this with their own experiences of groups.

Shirley's experience as a group member illustrated the role of group leaders: 'Pat was telling us about Martha and Mary, and then I completely took over. I said, "I'm sorry, Pat," but she said, "Oh no" . . . It's a different way of leading.'

Sue's criteria for choosing and training group leaders correspond with my recent research. Those who facilitate contextual theology need an attitude of solidarity with, and valuing of, those who live in the UK's UPA areas; they also need people and groupwork skills.

The church leaders had initiated groups, and then trusted them to operate without interference while remaining in the background as support. Sue explained, 'They (the church members) said that they would feel less intimidated if we weren't there', but she looked forward to the day when group leaders would be confident enough to allow her to be a participant.

Confidence-building was a consistent outcome throughout the process: for Sue, as a member of clergy; for group leaders; and for group members. Valuing people and their contributions affirmed them, and increased self-esteem. Sheila perhaps best sums this up: 'I was nervous to start with, but leading the group gave me the confidence to do things in front of a bigger group.'

Questions that emerge from this story in Hull may give a focus to continuing the conversations in other urban areas: In what ways do our approaches to learning and theology build or undermine the confidence of those in the congregation? How might they be better at building confidence? How can we move towards a place where those who live, worship and minister in urban areas learn together as we discover our contextual theology?

Notes

1 Canon Sue Sheriff has been linked with Unlock for more than ten years.
2 Unlock is a charity that provides training and resources for urban churches: Unlock, 336A City Road, Sheffield S2 1GA; www.unlock-urban.org.uk
3 Unlock's theological learning method is based on its mission statement:
   Unlocking real-life stories of urban people.
   Revealing the good news of the down-to-earth Christ.
   Releasing life-changing skills and confidence.
4 The Unlock method has its educational roots in David Kolb's theory of experiential learning ('The Process of Experiential Learning', in M. Thorpe *et al.* (eds), *Culture and Processes of Adult Learning*, Oxford University Press, 1993, p. 151): a learning process of moving from concrete experience, through reflective observation and abstract conceptualization to active experimentation.
5 Paulo Freire advocated listening carefully, identifying key issues for a community, and presenting people with a picture or story, offering the issue in a different situation (*Pedagogy of the Oppressed*, Penguin, 1972, p. 86). Unlock uses this notion to draw out people's real-life stories.

Preaching in an Urban World

Roger Sainsbury
Former Bishop of Barking

Believing urbanization can be of God

Aristotle is quoted as saying, 'Men came together in cities to live, but remained there to live the good life.' I believe it is important in our preaching today that we proclaim a belief that urbanization can be of God. The good life which God desires for all men and women can be experienced in the city. We need positive preaching about cities that expounds how they are part of God's plan for men and women and for the world. There is, however, a strong tradition in Christian preaching of denouncing the city in the tradition of the prophets (Jonah 1.2; Habakkuk 2.12).

John Chrysostom, in the fourth century, described as one who 'remains to this day a model for preachers in large cities', describes how, when 'we look over the city, we wept over it, as if it were on the eve of destruction'. Bishop Hugh Latimer, in the sixteenth century, the premier city preacher of the Reformation, began his famous sermon on the plough: 'Is there not reigning in London as much pride, as much covetousness, as much cruelty, as much oppression, and as much superstition, as was in Nebo? Yes, I think, and much more too. Therefore, I say, repent. O London; repent, repent.'

Yet Chrysostom and Latimer also preached positively about cities. Chrysostom, in a sermon in Antioch, proclaimed: 'There was nothing happier than our city', and Latimer commented positively about the care of the poor in his city: 'I heard very good report of London.'

Preachers such as Chrysostom and Latimer believed in cities, and their sermons condemning their sins were because of this belief and their desire for citizens to repent of those sins that spoilt the good life of their cities. In this it seems to me they were being true in their preaching to the revelation of God's plan for humanity revealed in the Scriptures. Jacques Ellul writes: 'When the Scriptures become more precise, it is always possible to describe the future under the aspect of a city.' I believe it is important that in our preaching today, we are much more positive about the city.

Preaching the gospel of faith

For the apostle Paul, preaching is at the heart of communicating the gospel of faith in the city (Romans 10.14–15). Commenting on these verses as a preacher, Olin Moyd says: 'In this age of secularism and relativism, or urbanisation and ghettoization, in an ironic way, the future of God is in the hands of preachers.' Drawing on the tradition of African-American preaching, he answers the question, 'How shall we preach?' in this way:

> The preaching was bibliocentric. It included elements of reproach, judgement, exhortation and promise. While the reproach in African-American preaching pointed to the sins and shortcomings of persons, it also addressed the corporate sins of an unjust and oppressive system.[1]

In my experience, preaching the gospel in our cities today will mean proclaiming God's victory in Christ over all that oppresses them, whether it is economic injustices or institutional racism. For Paul, the faith he preached had huge implications for the nature of society as we see in Romans 13.

Unmasking the powers that destroy faith

James Harris comments: 'Liberation preaching is preaching that challenges the established and prevailing social order, which is often the source of poverty, oppression, and injustice.'[2] Walter Wink links this type of preaching with the evangelistic zeal of the early Christians:

> The passion that drove the early Christians to evangelistic zeal was not fueled just by the desire to increase church membership or to usher people safely into a compensatory heaven after death. Their passion was fired above all by relief at being liberated from the delusions being spun over them by the Powers.[3]

I have seen at first hand, in my episcopal ministry, the evil forces of racism, economic exploitation and oppressive bureaucracies. Prophetic evangelism names these evil forces and powers. Prophetic preaching brings freedom in worship and a deeper commitment to follow Jesus.

Celebrating the new life of faith in urban communities

Frank Thomas writes that preaching has a very important role in creating communities of celebration:

> The Church can be understood as the *celebrative* community because celebration and thanksgiving are the natural response to the inner acceptance and appropriation of the Good News. After this response to the acceptance of the Good News, often one desires to become part of the community of people who have had the same experience of celebrations.[4]

In preaching missions in five London boroughs, we have always had as a climax of the mission a Celebration Rally, which has both celebrated the life of the local community and the grace of God revealed in Jesus Christ. We have seen people as a result want to join these communities of celebration and experience for themselves a living, transforming faith.

The Christian preacher is a direct heir of the Hebrew prophet. The prophets addressed the structural sins in society before calling individuals to repent (Amos 5.21–4; Isaiah 1.2–17). They presented a new vision of society as it should be before calling for individual faith (Isaiah 65—6). Jesus inherited this tradition (Matthew 6.33), as did the author of the Book of Revelation with his picture of the New Jerusalem (Revelation 21—2).

It is vital that we recover the social focus of the Scripture in our preaching today. Without the primary emphasis on social transformation through prophetic preaching, we will not see strong communities of faith in our urban areas. Individual faith will only flourish in the context of transformed communities.

Notes

1 Olin Moyd, *The Sacred Art* (Judson Press, 1995, p. 121).
2 James H. Harris, *Preaching Liberation* (Fortress, 1995, p. 12).
3 Walter Wink, *The Powers That Be* (Doubleday, 1998, p. 200).
4 Frank A. Thomas, *They Like to Never Quit Praisin' God* (United Church Press, 1997, p. 24).

Questions for Further Thought and Action

1 Use the model set out on page 42 for small groups to explore for themselves the meaning of stories from the Gospels for their own contexts.

2 Get copies of one of Unlock's packs and try it out with small groups in your congregation. See if you can get away from the clergy person dominating the process, and develop a group discovery process instead.

3 What are the issues in your locality that preaching needs to address? Does preaching have any role in evangelism? What is it?

5

Community

While we may concentrate on building up the Church as an alternative community of faith, we also need to relate it to the wider community of which it is part. The Church is after all the first instalment of the final regeneration of the whole universe.

This requires us to recognize and realize the existing links between Church and community. We need to seek the presence of the kingdom already in the community, as well as challenging the anti-kingdom which presents the lie of the kingdom's absence.

Greg Smith presents us with three case studies of churches in relationship with their community. He shows how Church can contribute to social cohesion through its inheritance of social capital.

Chris Erskine reflects on how local Christian communities can engage with their context practically, when they live out their values and act in humility.

Andy Dorton writes about his family's experience living on an outer estate. He shares movingly the pain and frustration of living Christ's life incarnationally alongside one's neighbours, identifying rather than preachifying.

Alan Craig describes how Christians have to mobilize politically at times. Even the policies of regeneration overtly intended to benefit the inner city too often actually oppose the interests of local residents, replacing local housing with gentrified new properties. In this situation, Christians have to adopt a resolutely, if uncomfortable, oppositional stance.

Building Community: Within and Without the Walls of the Church

Greg Smith

Research Fellow at the Centre for Institutional Studies in the University of East London, and freelance consultant with Credo Consultancy working for churches and volunteer groups. He currently serves on the Board of the local SRB6 Regeneration Partnership

Over the last 20 years I, with my family, have lived in two different cities and been in membership of three different churches. Each church has been committed to building community but each has struggled in different ways to make this a reality within and outside the walls of the church.

Church number one was a newly planted, basically charismatic fellowship with no building of its own. Its leadership was a core of like-minded committed Christian activists who saw mission as evangelism married with social transformation. They had a vision for evangelistic outreach centred on a council housing estate on the fringe of London Docklands, and social involvement in the wider life of the borough. There was considerable achievement in both areas, and over a decade there was a strong sense of community belonging both within the church membership and neighbourhood. However, there were struggles to bridge the cultural and educational gap between the social classes, and recurrent tensions over church discipline where individuals failed to keep traditional Christian standards of marital morality. Ten years ago there was a shaking out of core membership when a dozen key families, for their own reasons and without great conflict or broken relationships, moved to other churches and ministries.

Church number two was a more traditional Baptist church with a partially restored Victorian building opposite a mosque on a main road in one of the most multicultural areas in London. Over 30 years the white pastor had seen a church membership moving from majority white to 80 per cent Afro-Caribbean (traditional Baptists) and then to a more diverse fellowship in which zealous African and South Asian Christians played an increasingly significant role in leadership and ministry. Over the years various models of community service had been used, with an earlier focus on youth work in partnership with the council alongside family support and work with homeless people. Within the church the small miracle of fellowship between different ethnic groups was never simple, and was often disrupted by people moving out of the area. Work in the neighbourhood community was increasingly challenging as the church became more of a gathered congregation maintaining an evangelical witness in an area whose population became majority Muslim.

Church number three was an evangelical Anglican parish with a superb new building in a deprived neighbourhood in a city in the north of England. The congregation was lively and well mixed in terms of social class and age group, with a small minority of people from ethnic minorities. Some members, who travelled in from more affluent areas, and university students, found it difficult to relate to local working-class residents. Yet the local white population had a strong, conservative sense of local belonging which included for many a sense of Christian identity, perceived in contrast to the large (but minority) Hindu and Muslim communities. The parish ministry was strong among elders and children, with good links to the local primary school. However, there was much unrealized potential for community development work and the challenge of building bridges into the Asian communities in the neighbourhood.

The experience of these three churches suggests that the search for community is important but not straightforward. In Zygmunt Bauman's words, it is in part at least human beings 'seeking safety in an insecure world'.[1] Or, as Elizabeth Bounds writes, the role of the Church has elements both of 'coming together' and 'coming apart',[2] noting the glorious ambiguities in the latter phrase. The tendency is to use 'community' as a spray-can word painted on our public walls, or to give a sweet-smelling fragrance to the immediate environment, forgetting that aerosols also damage our social 'ozone layer'. There are, according to George Hillery,[3] at least 96 definitions of community, and although we all like the sound of the word, we can mean very different things when we use it. We cannot forget that definitions and boundaries of community are always contested, that communities build walls as well as affirm and support members, and only sometimes welcome strangers. Despite the teaching of the Law and the Prophets, the example of Jesus and the 'Koinonia' experience of the New Testament Church, often the Church fails to live up to its own community ideals.

A church is in danger when it becomes an inward-facing circle, a holy huddle with its back to the world. A church focused on mission can still be a circle of people with arms which at times are supportively linked, but needs to be facing outwards, with faces smiling in welcome, and hands willing to stretch out to draw others in. Recognizing the reality of rapid social change at local and global levels, our prayer, worship and action should be outward looking. In ministry, basic tools of outreach include social analysis, community service and community development.

In the UK and USA the current political climate offers many opportunities for partnership in social welfare and community work. Government has recently rediscovered the role of 'faith communities', especially in reaching parts that other services find hard to reach. However, the understanding of this notion of faith community leaves much to be desired, and practical policies are poorly developed and damaged by secular prejudice and religious illiteracy of many officials.

There is also a strong emphasis in government thinking on building up stocks of *social capital*, the networks and social trust that make for a community which may be more healthy and even more wealthy. Although social capital theory has problems, and is certainly not easy to measure by the statistical indicators that governments love, it is an important concept. Supportive networks are undoubtedly found as the result of the daily life and work of churches and other religious groups in inner-city areas, where other associations are weak or absent. Tactically at least, and for funding purposes not least, churches have much to gain by stressing their contribution to social capital.

More important perhaps is our potential contribution to *social cohesion*. Although this emphasis has deep roots in the sociology of Durkheim, the recent emphasis on the idea by government is more of a panic response. In the context of continuing urban deprivation, conflict and crime and in the wake of rioting in highly segregated cities in the north of England in 2001, and the global events that rocked the world in September the same year, local authorities were ordered to develop community cohesion strategies, to bring together all sections of the local population in co-operative and active participation for the common good. Here is a real opportunity for influence and ministry for churches in our inner cities, for three reasons:

1 The Church is one of the few places where people from different sections of the community meet together in fellowship and action. We have an experience to share.
2 In urban neighbourhoods where conflicts abound, governance is in chaos, people are alienated from power structures and every group promotes its own interests, the Church is still around, aware and involved, and can play a key role as an honest broker in wider debates.
3 The Church has the biblical vision of shalom as the realm where peace, justice and community health are perfectly realized. This vision can both transcend and inform the imperfect attempts of human institutions to create the cohesive and harmonious community which we all desire.

Notes

1 Z. Bauman, *Community, Seeking Safety in an Insecure World* (Polity Press, 2001).
2 E. M. Bounds, *Coming Together/Coming Apart: Religion, Community and Modernity* (Routledge, 1997).
3 G. Hillery, 'Definitions of Community; Areas of Agreement', *Rural Sociology* (1955, p. 117 ff.).

Community Development

Chris Erskine
Director of Development and Regeneration for the
Shaftesbury Society

Picture this: a relatively small but determined group of Christians in Doncaster really wants to reach out to the community. What do they do? First, a group goes onto the street to worship and preach. There is little response. Then they knock on people's doors and ask if they have anything to pray for. Again, there is limited response. Then they decide to do something very radical – *listen*. Yes, they listen to what local residents think the church could do.

Feedback from the community strongly identifies the need for an advice and support centre. So that's what they set up. The church embarks on a new journey, living out the gospel by demonstrating interest, support and care for people's lives. Over time, those involved discover that they are being changed by a growing desire to love those around them. They learn that change is a two-way street. Not only that: they also realize that God has been working in the community long before they set up the advice centre.

Nice fairy tale? No: just the signposts on the 15-year journey of Hexthorpe Methodist Church and the development of the Junction Advice Centre.

But what has this story got to tell us about Church and community development? Despite the recent flurry of interest in the relationship between Church and community, listening to the community still seems to be a challenge to many Christians. There remains a strong urge within the Church to keep telling communities that we have the answer to all of their problems. The difficulty with this is that we may completely miss the real questions, strengths and needs within a community.

Listening brings us to a place of understanding values. A key to developing communities is identifying *connecting values*. Connecting values can be concerns for particular people groups (i.e. older people), certain areas (i.e. use of public space) or single issues (i.e. crime). Finding out what people are concerned about, worried about, excited about, enables us to begin to share our lives with each other.

The identification of values brings us close to the passion of people. Passion, be it provoked by a sense of violation or hope, brings change. Value connection presents the opportunity for dialogue, appreciation and relationship. These opportunities can then lead to *building creatively* with and not for the community. The Christians in Doncaster began to understand and connect with their community issues. Building solutions around these connections brings the potential of meaningful ownership by the whole community. Ownership develops belonging, self-worth and significance – ownership builds communities.

The development of understanding and relationship also brings *value conversion*. 'Now we are getting to the real Christian bit,' I hear many thinking! However, the change process that can take place when Christians embark on a journey similar to those in Doncaster can raise many questions. Relationships with others will challenge our understanding of faith, mission, incarnation, evangelism and the cross, to name but a few examples. Often, we Christians need converting as much as anyone else. Let's look at an example:

> If anyone has material possessions and sees his brother in need but has no pity on him, how can the love of God be in him? (1 John 3.17)

These words are already powerful, but I believe that we have lost something in the translation. The words for 'material possessions' could read 'means of life of the world' or more simply 'life's resources', the point being that our Western response to need can always be to give from our material wealth. But our means of life should include our time, family, relationships, energy, etc.

Let me give a warning at this point: developing communities is contagious. It can get under your skin, into your head and change your life. If we allow it to, it will challenge our beliefs, dismantle our understanding of Church, and compel Christians to work with those in their communities and with each other. Indeed, Christians who seek to develop communities may find it increasingly difficult to understand why churches compete and duplicate activities. This leads them to explore how they can pool resources, redirect giving and meaningfully incarnate the fact that they are *one*. In a nutshell, if Christians are going to develop communities, we need to develop our unity. This means sacrifice: we must lay down our lives, names, ministries and denominations for the love of this world. This suggestion may cause some concern, but think of Jesus:

> Who, being in very nature God, did not consider equality with God something to be grasped, but made himself nothing, taking the very nature of a servant, being made in human likeness. And being found in appearance as a man, he humbled himself and became obedient to death – even death on a cross! (Philippians 2.6–8)

Diversity and flexibility in approach should grow from *connecting values not different dogma*. The inward-looking duplication and competition which often characterizes local churches will need to change. Christians are fragments of the fullness – we need each other. We all see through a glass dimly.

Finally, although the Church may have retreated from having a meaningful presence in many areas of this country, God clearly has not. People pray, believe and receive. Sometimes there is more manifest faith in the estate than there is at the Eucharist! Humility alone will let us find out just how true this is. The only way this will happen is if we begin where this article began, with listening to God and one another.

'On' the Estate

Andy Dorton
Social Responsibility Officer in Hull and the East Riding for the Diocese of York, North Bransholme, Hull

Our family, two adults, two children (now 14 and 12) have lived here in North Bransholme for ten years. Andy works for the Church of England as a Social Responsibility Officer. Liz is a freelance puppeteer. We moved here by choice from a large vicarage near the centre of Hull. We decided that the end of our earth was this estate (and our earth is obviously Hull). The estate was built in the 1970s; there was a sign on the one road, which said 'Bransholme: Works in Progress'. It said a lot, mainly that the place was never finished, and it still isn't.

We do not intend to theorize: this is where we live and love. In many ways we are still basically 'middle class'; in some ways though, we are now not. Little words say a lot; why do people live *on* council estates, not *in* them? We are consciously using the 'in' word. Very few people were ever here by choice. Most were put 'on' here by an allocations policy. There was no choice. We had a choice; we were different.

We are hardly, for these purposes, 'C of E'; we go mainly to an Anglican church in Bransholme; there is no church of any physical sort on North Bransholme for its 2,200 houses and 7,200 people. Andy is not ordained; we are not technically 'in ministry'. While you could say we have one, it is not a term we'd employ ourselves or round here; but then neither is 'Church'.

Let's talk about children

The problem with Jesus is he never had kids: claim he understands all our temptations if you like, but he never had kids. Some people were angry at us for bringing our children here; for imposing 'our' values on 'our' children. Andy was clear that not only would our kids go to the primary school at the back of our house, but that they'd go to the extremely poor performing secondary. Andy's view is this: they are not 'our values' and they are not 'our kids'. We hope they are God's values, and we believe they are God's children.

Liz has coped with much greater anxiety about the quality of education and the social stuff of school life by learning what 'Pray without ceasing . . .', 'Do not worry . . .' and 'Let each day's troubles . . .' really mean. And Liz has got organized: she has worked in the school, adding elements that pressured teachers had to give up on; and she gets people together to pray regularly from all denominations. She has seen some extraordinary changes in the schools' culture and children's experiences as a result.

What gets us down?

The uniformity; the poor old rose bushes; the empties; the constant wilful destruction; losing neighbours. Estates don't develop organically; they are designed on paper, where they no doubt look great. In practice, they are of uniform constructions, sizes, layouts and so forth. The bit of colour came from the municipal roses; de-headed hundreds of times, they soldier on unless older children have trampled them completely or they've been undermined by little children discovering the sandy soil that was originally put around them.

After we had been here a couple of years, the cataclysmic downturn in Hull's population began to bite here first. Initially, the turn-over (or 'churn') of tenants increased dramatically, then increasingly they were not replaced at all. Now, 300 sound 1970s good-sized houses have already been demolished and another 400 remain empty.

On a large new private development 'next door' (but at a defensible social and physical distance of course), people 'escaping' estates buy a same-roomed but more cramped house with mini-garden, but with car-worship space attached, for £50,000–£70,000 when ours is now worth £5,000. Why? Because people have swallowed the Thatcher line: council estate tenant, second-class citizen; owner-occupier, better-class citizen. And Blair has done nothing to reverse this socially corrosive truism.

So what are we doing here?

When we came here, we had no agenda. We knew there was no manifestation of 'Christian community' here and we wanted to be part of one, and we have been falteringly 'successful' in that aim. A group of us meets every two weeks; we do bits of traditional stuff, but rarely in a traditional form and we drink/rant/chunter a lot afterwards. If you'd like to research what a 'celidh house' was, you'll get an idea, then add free book room, art showroom, bike repair shop and other stuff.

One of the good things about the churn was that quickly we became established residents. And when things are changing all around, if you are a decent constant, you are more easily accepted, along with what you can offer – not just among neighbours, but in local organizations, residents or action groups.

We thought we'd be at the near-birth of this estate; it was only a generation old. It was unformed, unrooted, uncared-for; it had relatively few established social and other networks. We thought we could be part of its childhood and adolescence at least; maybe grow old with it. As it is, we could have come for its dying.

Should we be fighting for something as ill-conceived as this was in the first place; can everybody else (it feels like) be wrong? *Yes.* Ordinary people make their own history, usually in struggle. We live in a well-designed, microcommunity-enhancing square of houses around a car-free patch of grass. We have designed a new Jerusalem: a spacious place with room to grow in (salvation); we will be rebuilders of streets with walls; a good place for the 'fatherless' and those who know that the Blair world's values are not for them. There is a lot more government-inspired opportunity around for local people to take control over our corporate destiny, and many of us are going to make the most of that.

We believe that everything is redeemable

Today we are painting the 'white boards' (covering the windows on the empty houses) on another square as a pilot for the estate: we have thousands of empty canvases and some of us residents have decided that we will say that there is life here (celebrating our wildlife and greenery and that we can see the sunrise and sunset from our ten-metre height at the top of Hull) and that it will be a sign of the re-invention of the estate over the years to come.

There may never be a 'church' here in traditional form: we hope not. We believe that the good news God on the side of those pushed to the edge will be revealed.

We have tried to take the Bible seriously; it says go to the ends of the earth. One of those 'ends' in our society is most certainly the outer estate. We can't believe God wants all his name-owning salt and light in the suburbs. We think it should take a special dispensation not to go and do likewise.

Political Involvement:
Local Resistance to Regeneration Policies

Alan Craig
Director of Mayflower Family Centre, Canning Town, east London

'The whole thing stinks,' shouted a local resident at a packed and angry public meeting organized by Newham Council in early 2001. 'You want to move us out so that you can get the yuppies in.' I felt angry too as I listened to council officers explain their housing regeneration project.

Land values had rocketed in our neighbourhood since the gleaming new nearby Canning Town Station opened in 1999. Our isolated, deprived inner-city council estate suddenly had access to the equally new Jubilee Underground Line extension and Docklands Light Railway, and consequently it now had easy links to Canary Wharf, the City and the West End. Overnight our shunned Keir

Hardie estate found itself sitting on immensely valuable land, and the council wanted to use this as leverage for private developers to regenerate the housing stock.

Nothing wrong with that, and indeed the council might have been commended for seizing a unique golden opportunity to improve housing for the long-suffering local community. Working with the local people, they could develop a bright new future for the neighbourhood. The government's Urban White Paper published in November 2000 had highlighted the way that sustainable and enlightened regeneration should be undertaken in the twenty-first century:

> A clear message from the regeneration initiatives of the last 30 years is that real sustainable change will not be achieved unless local people are in the driving seat. It is not enough to consult people; they must be fully engaged in the process from the start, and everybody must be included. This is both the mark of a decent society and plain good sense.

The problem was that this was not the council's method; they seemed uninterested in both decency and good sense. Instead brutally and unilaterally they had announced from the Town Hall that 1,900 families were to be decanted from their homes on the estate and that only 425 would be allowed back. Furthermore, the few who had exercised the right to buy their council property would, if necessary, be subject to compulsory purchase orders in order to force them out of their homes. The clear intention of the council was to free up as much land as possible so that private developers could build private property for more prosperous private residents. It was thought that thereby they would make the area into a more desirable and socially mixed location.

The response was bitter and furious. Letters were written to the *Newham Recorder*, a Residents' Action Group was set up, 350 people attended a protest meeting in the Mayflower chapel in the centre of the estate, and there was a noisy demonstration outside the Town Hall.

The response was also one of distress and confusion. No indication was given about when or to where residents would have to move. Elderly people who had survived Hitler's blitz on the nearby docks were sleepless at the thought of being removed from their homes.

Single mums worried about finding new support for bringing up the kids in a strange neighbourhood. Residents had no idea whether to continue with plans to improve their homes with replacement kitchens if their residences were soon to be pulled down.

The Mayflower Family Centre, a church and community centre founded in 1958 by David Sheppard, the former England cricket captain and now retired Bishop of Liverpool, was in the middle of the regeneration area, although fortunately its own site was excluded from the plans.

Also, following attacks by an ultra-left group within Newham Council on Mayflower's Christian equal opportunities policy, there had been a withdrawal of all local authority funding in the early 1990s. Therefore by the grace of God the Centre had become one of very few significant voluntary sector organizations in the borough that was now completely independent financially.

The stage was set for Mayflower to take a lead in opposing the Council's top-down and, in my view, profoundly un-Christian way of undertaking regeneration, while nonetheless welcoming housing regeneration itself as necessary and indeed long overdue.

As Director of Mayflower, I wrote a number of blunt letters to the local newspaper, and in one edition received the dubious accolade of vicious personal attacks in its columns both from the Leader of the Council and from the senior journalist in the borough. However, one method of opposition had to be undertaken outside the Mayflower. As a registered charity, the Centre could not be involved in any political or election activity. For some years I had seen the need for overt Christian witness in politics, and in the 1998 local elections a friend and I stood as independent 'Christian Democrats' in the ward that surrounds Mayflower. We surprised ourselves and others by beating the BNP, Liberal Democrats and Conservatives, and coming second to Labour.

Then providentially, following the death of a councillor in the next-door ward, a by-election was called two months after the announcement of the regeneration project, in March 2001. By that time I had helped form a new national political party, the Christian People's Alliance. I campaigned as their candidate and as the candidate opposed to the Council's regeneration methods. 'Labour's Fortress Threatened By A Christian Soldier' proclaimed headlines over a full-page article in the *London Evening Standard*, but I lost – albeit by only 58 votes!

Next came the local elections in May 2002. Uniquely in Britain, Labour in Newham had secured all 60 council seats in the local elections of both 1994 and 1998. Historically, Canning Town has been bedrock Labour territory since time immemorial. The area elected Keir Hardie as the first-ever Labour MP in 1896 (our estate is named after him), and it has sent only Labour Councillors to the Town Hall since 1912 when current records began.

Again I campaigned against the council. As well as the popularity of this campaign theme, I had three other factors in my favour: I was identified with the Mayflower, which is well respected in the neighbourhood and has been involved in the lives of many locals; I myself have lived in Canning Town for over two decades and become personally recognized in the community; and my Christian political label was a positive and unique selling point among the growing ethnic minority in the area.

On election night I came top of the poll in Canning Town South ward. Elsewhere the Labour steamroller again flattened all the opposition, so that the party gained all the other 59 seats. I became the lone, not-always-loyal, Opposition. It was a small political earthquake, but it was a sign of what can happen when a party loses touch with the interests and aspirations of its natural supporters.

The residents' campaign against the council's approach to the regeneration – of which my political activities have been only part – has scored some successes and challenged borough bosses to modify their approach. By using the media and motions at council meetings, I have even forced the Town Hall to consider a ballot of the residents. But the bosses still hold all the cards, and at the time of writing they continue to bulldoze through their top-down imposed scheme.

The locals' resigned shrug tells it all. We may end up with a scheme that has attractive buildings. But it will not be owned or appreciated by many of the local people who should have been the first to benefit. It is a sadly missed opportunity.

———————————

Questions for Further Thought and Action

1 Undertake an audit of your community. What are its strengths and weaknesses? Who are the movers and shakers? What are the current needs, concerns and interests of different groups of people?

2 Identify the people and the projects which make for the well-being of your community. How can your church celebrate and affirm this?

3 Where is the salt, light and leaven needed in your area? How can Christian people together make a difference here?

4 What are those policies and practices, of local or national government, which are undermining your local community? How might your church, with others, stand against these?

6

Race

One issue which occurs throughout many of these pieces is that of race and racism. How is the Church to act in the face of injustice, prejudice and institutional racism in society at large or in its local vicinity? How should we respond to the presence of refugees among us? Or, how can a local church address these issues as they affect its fellowship, in leadership, power allocation, and influence in the congregation? Is it possible to have a truly multicultural Church? Or is that a chimera? What is the place of the monoethnic Church?

Wale Hudson Roberts addresses the wider issue of whether the Church is relevant to an increasingly multicultural society. He challenges the traditional notion of integration as uniformity, and calls us to frame a congregation which values difference and does not reduce everyone to sameness.

Sheila Garvin describes her involvement with refugees. She evokes the difficulties which they face in settling here, but also points out the joys and blessings she has received from her work. She does not, however, give way to an easy-going sentimentality, but is scathing about the failure of many Christians to respond to this problem and to resist the demonization of 'asylum-seekers'.

Andy Bruce's account demonstrates how a particular church has transitioned into a multicultural church. Again, he does not pull his punches, and states clearly how difficult that has been in practice. Hard questions of power and control have to be confronted in order to move forward. Multiculturalism is more a matter of journey than arrival.

In contrast, **Robert Tang** demonstrates how a monocultural church has met the distinct cultural and missionary needs of a particular ethnic group. He indicates, however, that culture is never static. Generational change presents its own dilemmas, as younger people identify less with their parents' heritage. They occupy a cultural border zone, which poses fresh challenges to ecclesial shape in this century.

The Multicultural Society, the Multicultural Church

Wale Hudson Roberts

Racial Justice Co-ordinator for the Baptist Union of Great Britain

Sixty per cent of the population in some areas of Britain is comprised of individuals from minority ethnic backgrounds. Furthermore, Britain has one of the highest proportions of mixed race relationships: 50 per cent of black men and a third of Asian men are now dating white partners. Even though their proportion in terms of population is only 6 per cent, South Asian Britons make up 20 per cent of hospital doctors, most of whom came fully trained and have saved the NHS £300 million as a result. Better still, Indian food now has a turnover which is higher than coal, steel and ship-building combined. Prince Charles eloquently summarized the burgeoning contribution that black and minority ethnics have made to Britain when he said: 'Their contribution is incredibly wide and varied – from the economy, politics, public service and the law, medicine, the arts and even our cooking. It is a contribution which today forms part of our national identity, and it adds immeasurably to the richness and creativity of modern Britain.'

Even though Prince Charles' statement has much truth to it, lurking beneath the surface of this growing multicultural phenomenon remain inequality and exclusion. This is clearly exemplified in the British corridors of power. For example, out of 651 MPs currently in post, only 12 are from the minorities. Likewise, there are presently no High Court Judges, or national newspaper editors, and a paucity of high-ranking police officers from minority ethnic backgrounds. This glaring inequity was bravely commented upon by Tony Blair who said: 'We cannot be a beacon to all the world unless the talents of all the people shine through. Not one black High Court Judge; not one black Chief Constable or Permanent Secretary, not one black Army Officer above the rank of Colonel. Not one Asian either.'

In my opinion, this overt absence of justice is symptomatic of an institutionally racist society. Direct racial discrimination continues to be experienced by a significant section of the black and minority population. The worst affected are Bangladeshis, Pakistanis and young Caribbean men. The most recent Policy Studies Institute survey shows that 250,000 Caribbeans and Asians experience racial harassment every year. A report on racial harassment and violence by the All Party Parliamentary Group on Race and Community concluded: 'It would hardly be an exaggeration to say that one in every two Afro-Caribbean and Asian families suffered directly or indirectly from the effects of racial incidents in 1999.'

Stemming the tide then of a society that is inexorably moving down the racialist stretch, oblivious to the resistance from the voluble card-carrying multiculturalist, is by no means an easy feat. However, Roy Jenkins hit the nail on the head in his speech on integration on 29 May 1966 when he said:

> Integration does not mean the loss by immigrants of their own national characteristics and culture. I do not think we need in this country a 'melting pot'. It would deprive us of most of the positive benefits of immigration that I believe to be very great indeed. I define integration therefore, not as a flattening process of assimilation, but as an equal opportunity, accompanied by cultural diversity in an atmosphere of mutual tolerance.

Arguably, one of the few institutions able to demonstrate the multicultural agenda actively should be the Church. The multicultural Church, for all its popularity and ubiquity, however, is still without a coherent definition. It is nevertheless unequivocal in its rejection of cultural discrimination and insensitivity, and clear in its commitment to cultural diversity and difference, believing that all cultures are equally valuable and equally deserving of our respect.

An illustration from the world of music may help us translate the multicultural theory into practice. Every instrument plays its appropriate theme and melody in the whole symphony. Similarly in church, each ethnic group is a distinct instrument with its own temper and culture. These give it its melody, as well as its harmony and dissonance, not to forget irritating discords, all of which contribute to the symphony's unique sound.

Of course I am aware that not everyone will subscribe to this interpretation of a multicultural utopia, though I am sure that as Christians we will agree that integration matched with freedom of cultural expression is a biblical imperative as well as an essential precondition for a democratic Church.

The Gospels, for example, present the ministry of Jesus as radically inclusive in the face of organized religion's exclusivity. He experienced racism because of his perceived origins in Nazareth and his cross-cultural ministry among Gentiles. This, and more, whipped up the heightening prejudice towards Jesus and his ministry. Yet Jesus' instinct to be inclusive was not without its limits. In John 4 Jesus breaks social convention by speaking to a woman, and non-Jew, without compromising his moral criticism of serial polygamy or his belief in the absolute holiness of God. And so, while encouraging the Samaritan woman to play a key role in the symphony, Jesus is not oblivious to her discords.

I am the first to acknowledge that the complex process of disentangling the negotiable from the non-negotiable is often problematic. However, the fact that some cultural distinctions are insignificant does not mean that they are to be disregarded. Just as the Holy Spirit worked through different languages to reach the crowds at Pentecost, so Paul was willing to use cultural distinctives as a tool for gospel communication.

And so for Tony Blair's Britain to be truly multicultural, both Church and society need to adhere to the radical words of James H. Cone on integration: 'If integration means accepting the white man's style, his values or his religion, then the minority culture must refuse. There is nothing to integrate. On the other hand, if integration means that each man meets the other on equal footing, with neither possessing the ability to assert the rightness of his style over the other, then mutual meaningful dialogue is possible. Biblically this may be called the Kingdom.'

'I Was a Stranger'

Sheila Garvin

A social worker in Wolverhampton, working with a Methodist-based project in an inner-city district, where she is engaged in a wide range of community activities

I have spent most of my working life, of 30 years, living in inner-city multiethnic communities working mainly with Hindu and Sikh people from India. I love city life and have grown to love Indian food, as has much of the population, become familiar with customs, attended numerous weddings, and worshipped with the Asian Christian community. The down side of inner-city life is crime and the fear of crime. I have found it beneficial to identify with the problems of my neighbours, and getting alongside them has been a major aim of my work.

When I was younger I did a lot of youth work and worked with inner-city deprived young people. I attempted to draw them into church life but without much success, as it was too much of a cultural shock. They could not cope with the worship, and their expectations were not met. The Methodist Church did give opportunities for young black people, and some benefited from their training who are now in leadership positions in church.

Many people from other faiths who professed faith in Christ are now nowhere near a church. The predominantly white-led Church could not give them an alternative family. It is very difficult for young Asian people brought up in our society to fit into a traditional Asian church or a mainly white-led church, although ethnic churches have to some extent met their need.

I later moved from a welfare position to one of advocacy, so that the community could claim what was their right. I became involved in housing issues, immigration, benefits and credit unions. I became involved in local politics as a way to meet these needs, and was active in a wide range of local issues.

My working life changed three years ago when a group of young men came to my office one Monday morning asking for help in how to use an electricity meter. They had already found the Social Services office and had been re-directed to me. They had come from Kent on Friday evening in three coaches and been allocated various houses. They were not shown how to use a slot meter and so had been unable to wash or cook over the weekend. I had been introduced to asylum-seekers from Afghanistan who had been dispersed to Wolverhampton.

Over the weeks I learnt a lot. I knew where Afghanistan was on the map and I started my journey in learning about the needs of asylum-seekers, most of whom were young men and mainly Muslim. The initial dispersal meant that the community was not prepared for them, and so it was learning 'on the hoof' for voluntary and statutory agencies alike.

English classes were set up, clothing obtained, and social events run on a Saturday afternoon in local churches. The men were lonely, poor and very isolated. However I soon discovered that many were very gifted. Some learnt English quickly, found ways of earning money, were very hospitable to newcomers, and enjoyed exploring nightclubs and bars which had been forbidden territory in Afghanistan.

Many however found it extremely difficult. Due to the Taliban many had not been able to go school and so found English hard. They were separated from their wives and families, and were socially isolated due to lack of money to participate in society. Many bore the physical scars of war, which would never heal. I have spent a lot of time completing forms for charitable help so that they had some extra cash for basics. At that time they were receiving vouchers which could only be cashed in supermarkets such as Safeway and Sainsbury's which did not supply halal meat. Haircuts, phone cards and televisions could not be bought from the weekly £10 cash, and few had been able to bring money with them.

When families started arriving it was easier for churches to assist. The children needed toys and clothes, and women and children fitted more easily into the social activities of the church life. Attempts have been made to get asylum-seekers linked to individuals, but this is not always easy due to language difficulties.

I met with missionaries who had worked in Afghanistan, who helped me understand more about the culture. I probably made lots of mistakes, but was forgiven (or so I think) for my willingness to befriend and help if I could. I washed the clothes of two young women who had worn them from Afghanistan to Wolverhampton, only for them to have them stolen due to my carelessness. They said 'No problem' and I felt awful that they had lost what had been very valuable possessions.

The town centre Assemblies of God has established a Sunday afternoon session for asylum-seekers when they play games, offer some food and chat. They have found that they have attracted many from the Roma communities, and that they are having to cope with the emotional aspects of deportation, having built up a relationship with them, as well as the different attitudes to other people's property which can be appropriated from time to time.

Some churches have found asylum-seekers from non-Christian backgrounds joining them and seeking baptism. It is not always easy to discern if the reason is to assist their asylum application by avoiding being returned to a country which is not sympathetic to Christians.

Most churches in inner-city areas have benefited from asylum-seekers from Africa who have joined them as regular members of the congregations, and in a few cases ethnic churches have been set up to meet particular language needs. I met a Bible translator from the Congo on my travels and wondered if he could find employment in this area in the UK.

My relationship with asylum-seekers has changed as they have become settled. Some have been permitted to remain in the UK and so there are problems of employment, health, education, etc. I have found many are now troubled with their experiences which include rape, torture, beatings. These are evidenced by inability to sleep, headaches, physical pain, depression and anxiety. They are being referred to the various mental health services which are poor at the best of times, even for the host community. I have been working with a counsellor who has particular skills in trauma counselling to meet this need, but it is overwhelming. I hope that it will be possible to do more in the future.

On the whole, children are doing very well at school, as many are coming from middle-class backgrounds and are highly motivated. Children from Romany families are often less motivated and there are problems with attendance. It is worrying that children in emergency accommodation find it hard to access education, as schools are reluctant to have them because they are likely to be there for a short time – even though that can be many months.

My spiritual life has been enriched by my friendship with those of many faiths or no faith. I have appreciated the hospitality of those who have very little in the world's terms, and been humbled that I who have so much do not give so willingly.

Look: A Multicultural Church!

Andy Bruce
Pastor of Mansfield Road Baptist Church, Nottingham

This is not a multicultural church! We would love to be one, and have made several important strides in that direction; you could say we are on a journey, and have passed some notable milestones – but we have not yet arrived!

At some point in the past five years, Mansfield Road Baptist Church became a black-majority church. It is important to note here that both the concept and the terminology are slippery. Even the simple matter of observing numbers – seeing who is in the majority – is by no means self-evident. It is comparatively recently that the *membership* became majority black. However, black Christians had been a majority in the congregation (at least on some occasions) for some time before that. It is also the case that over perhaps the last 20 years, most of this church's pastoral and evangelistic contacts have been from the black community. But in a formal sense, these things do not make a church 'majority black', far less one that is multicultural.

When, from the late 1950s onwards, initially as a trickle, later a steady stream, Jamaicans started making their home in this church, the existing congregation began a process of accommodating these newcomers with their distinct cultural identity. There were a few tensions, but in general the quality of *hospitality* offered was sufficient for many Christians arriving from the Caribbean to become part of the church family here and begin to put down spiritual roots. Their absorption was aided by the fact that many Jamaican Baptists were 'more English than the English' and had no desire to challenge the white middle-class version of traditional Christianity they encountered in this church. They delighted simply in being allowed to be part of it. There were others who would have valued greater freedom and were frustrated by the typically English reserve that predominated, but the benefits generally outweighed the disadvantages, and most of them stayed. In time, two black members were elected as deacons, and for many, both white and black, this token presence in the church leadership was evidence of full acceptance and integration. Surely the church was now multicultural?

This pattern of a traditional English Baptist church where things were done decently and in order, according to white middle-class values, with a congregation that included a growing number of Jamaican and black-British members, continued to be the norm through the 1960s and 1970s. It was multiracial, but not multicultural. In the early 1980s, ten years after the Charismatic Movement caused a stir in many 'mainstream' churches, such was the self-confidence of this church that worship style and spiritual renewal became key issues for Mansfield Road. Changes in the conduct of worship during this period were not dramatic, but were certainly significant. An important symbol of change was the replacement of the antediluvian choir with a more modern 'music group' which included a majority of black singers. Alongside this there was an active and successful attempt to involve more black members in public worship, including leading whole services. (This process is described in more detail by my colleague the Revd Anne Davies in her article, 'A Hard Road to Travel', *Baptist Ministers' Journal*, July 2002.) Through these developments the visible 'face' of the church began to change and the number of black attenders increased still further. Surely there was now clear evidence of a multicultural church emerging?

By the end of the 1990s, leadership had become the most pressing focus of change in the church. Two long-serving ministers had moved on and more youthful models were appointed. At the same time, a whole generation of senior leaders in the church quite naturally came to the end of their tenure, creating space into which new leadership candidates could emerge. An in-house 'Black Baptist Support Group' had highlighted the fact that leadership in the church was still predominantly white, and had begun actively to encourage more black church members into leadership roles. The proportion of black deacons increased, one of whom was elected to chair the Property Committee, and the church employed its first black member of staff – the manager of the new Family Centre. The balance of power was shifting, and this did not go unnoticed. Hushed and guilty voices were occasionally heard to say, 'You have to be black to count for anything around here.'

Suppressed prejudice, occasionally bubbling to the surface in unguarded comments, condescending acceptance that leaves the glass ceiling intact, and cultural quietism that ignores slights and overlooks false assumptions and generalizations, are clearly major obstacles to genuine community. These underlying attitudes among both black and white members, the protective desire of a 'close' fellowship to keep everything cosy at any price, had to be exposed if progress was to be made, and this proved to be a costly and demanding business. It is not for the faint-hearted! This church had to go through a long and painful process of learning to confront unacceptable attitudes and behaviour. Its ministers, both implacably committed to empowering the black members, had also to learn how to censure and challenge them when necessary. Theology, pastoral practice, church administration, finance, social and political engagement, ecumenism – all these had to be re-examined. Although the road was indeed hard, surely the fact that the church had the stomach to tackle such uncomfortable issues – and it did – proved that a truly multicultural church was on its way.

We now have a mission statement that explicitly declares our commitment to be inclusive, together with a comprehensive raft of policy and procedure documents to back it up. We have successfully challenged the automatic right of white professional newcomers to the church to become the leading members ahead of black people joining at the same time. We have been through the trauma of being accused of not addressing racial injustice in our midst, and have emerged from that test humbler and more realistic. But our ministers are still white, our black worship leaders continue to lead in a 'white' style, written rather than verbal communication remains the norm, and the congregation resolutely considers any song in a language other than English to be a novelty!

I believe that we *are* a witness to our city in our determination to avoid the usual polarization between different communities. The congregation now includes significant minorities from several countries apart from the British and Jamaican majority groups. An African congregation meets weekly on our premises and our Family Centre is increasingly winning the trust of our Pakistani neighbours. The signs are good: I have no doubt that God wants us to be a multicultural church – and I pray that one day soon we will become one!

Planting a Chinese Congregation in Hounslow: A Decade of Mission

Robert Tang
Pastor of the Chinese Church in London

The sending church's vision

The Chinese Church in London (CCiL) is an ethnic church of about 800 registered members made up of eight congregations with four in central London, one in Finsbury Park, one in Croydon, one in Hounslow and one in Colindale. The vision of CCiL is to see Chinese congregations formed in the various regions of Greater London Area as it is their calling to bring Christ to Chinese people in London. In 1993, a mission was launched into the South West region of the Greater London Area (GLA) focusing on the town of Hounslow as there was a thriving Saturday Chinese School of 500 pupils. Furthermore, a number of church members already lived in that area.

The local Chinese School's support

The Chinese School attracted many Chinese families from the areas surrounding Hounslow as far as Slough in Berkshire. It therefore constituted an excellent outreach target. The mission activities included a Summer Club for the children and workshops for the parents. This took place when the Chinese School had their summer break. The people were also invited to evangelistic meetings. These events took place at the local school premises where the Saturday Chinese School was based. The Chinese School continues to serve the community from the same premises to this day.

The local church's support

Hounslow Evangelical Church offered the use of their premises for weekly Bible study, monthly fellowship meeting and eventually weekly worship service. Those who responded to the gospel were followed up and nurtured there. Other churches in Hounslow also encouraged us as they had great difficulty in reaching the Chinese themselves owing to the language and cultural obstacles. The newly founded Chinese congregation was to see itself not only as one of the congregations of Chinese Church in London but also as a member of the greater Body of Christ in Hounslow. As such, the Chinese congregation takes part in the joint activities organized by an association of churches bearing the name of 'Hope for Hounslow'.

The sending church's support

The sending church graciously awarded the new congregation with one pastor though a part of his time was taken up with its corporate administration. A few members from the mother church who do not live locally in Hounslow also committed themselves to serve in the new congregation for a number of years. This was necessary to build up the local leadership base. The new congregation is nourished by quality joint activities organized by the mother church, such as a cross-cultural mission conference, an Easter retreat and a Summer Bible School. The new congregation adopts the practices of CCiL without having to re-invent the wheel every time, whether in pastoral or administration issues.

The people profile

According to the 2001 Census, there are 1,842 Chinese in Hounslow. Kingston has 2,026 Chinese. Richmond has 1,299 and Slough has 349. The total amounts to over 5,000 in the south-west region of the Greater London Area.

The Chinese people encountered in the course of the ministries have the following profiles: catering trade, professionals, students, asylum-seekers, retirees, children and teens. The dominant profile is that of families. The wives have been more responsive to the gospel than the husbands.

The language of the children and teens is English, whereas the language of the parents is Cantonese, a popular dialect in southern China. The language of the asylum-seekers and students from China is Mandarin. On the whole, the Mandarin-speaking Chinese are the most responsive to the gospel.

The local ministries

Sunday Worship is held in the afternoon at Hounslow Evangelical Church. The service is preceded by a prayer meeting and followed by an Adult Sunday School. The children take part in the first part of the worship, which is conducted in Chinese with English interpretation. Then they leave for their own classes which are delivered in English. At that point, the worship turns into Chinese only.

During weekdays, the care network extends over three District Care Groups. Friendship evangelism is encouraged. During festive seasons, such as Chinese New Year and Christmas, a concerted effort is made to hold evangelistic meetings. There is also an organized visitation programme to visit all the Chinese in Hounslow and the surrounding districts.

Reflection

It took combined support from the sending church, local church and local ethnic group to establish the congregation.

The dynamic balance between reaching out to new people and building up the existing people must be delicately maintained. The purpose of the sending church, the Chinese Church in London, is helpful here – to Chinese people we bring Christ in whom we grow together to be sent out to serve God in the world. The vision to evangelize and to multiply must be kept alive.

Similarly, the dynamic balance between building up the Body of Christ and engaging in social concern must also be maintained. A young congregation should concentrate on evangelism and building itself up. In its more mature years, it should plant its own new congregation, like the sending church. It should also actively engage in social concern in the locality.

Leadership development is a key to the long-term future. Equally, the issue of the long-term future of the next generation Chinese (British-born Chinese) who are English-speaking must be addressed. They would need to develop through the following three stages:

1 Worship with their parents.
2 Have their own English-speaking youth congregation.
3 Integrate into other local non-ethnic churches.

The congregation should grow towards autonomy. With the blessing of the sending church, it should develop into an independent church. With gratitude, it would voluntarily contribute back to the sending church. With great hope for the future, it would actively engage in mission and social concern locally and globally, like its parent church.

Questions for Further Thought and Action

1 (a) How can your church celebrate and affirm the racial mix in your community and congregation, in ways that affirm the uniqueness of each, resist superficiality, oppose racism and make for harmony?
  (b) Contact local voluntary or statutory bodies which deal with racism and seek ways of working together.

2 Find out if there are any refugees and asylum-seekers in your community and congregation. Who is working with them? What are their basic needs? How can your church best help?

3 (a) If you are in a white-led or mixed congregation, seek out the minority ethnic churches in your locality. If you belong to a predominantly ethnic minority church, seek out churches which are mainly white or comprise people from other ethnic groups. Pray about and discuss ways of making links.
  (b) If you are in a multicultural congregation, analyse who has the power in your church. How can you ensure that leadership reflects the make-up of the membership?

4 Identify minority ethnic communities in your locality where there is no Christian presence. Contact one of the Christian agencies which specialize in mission among this people group and explore partnership with them in developing appropriate ministries.

7

Cultural Change

The traditional binary pattern of 'race relations' in this country has been replaced by a kaleidoscopic mix of shifting *ethne* – some moving out, some arriving in, the inner city. A constant flow of new and old, people groups, languages, cultures and lifestyles, mirroring the flow of capital across the globe.

Christians need to understand this shape-shifting, changeling postmetropolis. Not only that, but as Christians we too are part of the mix, adding to its religio-cultural complexity, with all our diverse traditions and ethno-economic class/strata divisions.

This overlapping parallelogram of urban lifestyles embraces more than the ethnic – in the postmodern city construct, there are many micro-communities and social belongings. Our contributors, however, have focused more on the changing nature of identity formation, learning and belonging.

Graham Routley gives us a flavour of the ethnic diversity, and lists a few snapshots of Abrahamic multiethnic blessing. In a world sovereignly ruled by God, such variety must be God-given, a cause for thanksgiving to the Creator of all peoples.

Mark Perrott shares his experience as an incomer to the inner city. He describes his journey of faith, the lessons he has learned and the openings he has seen for involvement in mission among the poorest and most marginalized.

Richard Springer writes about the experience of the second and third generation within the Afro-Caribbean community. He articulates their attempt to negotiate identity between a traditional church culture and a hostile host culture, and shows that the creative resources that sustained their fathers and mothers still remain through the Divine Spirit.

Finally, **Wagih Abdelmassih** gives an account of how Britain is viewed by Christians recently arrived – their expectations and frustrations – especially when coming from a home situation where Christians are persecuted.

Pluralism and Diversity

Graham Routley

Team Leader for Interserve's Urban Vision (formerly Ministry Among
Asians in Britain), a cross-cultural mission agency

To whom does the city belong? The once clear and unambiguous
answer is now less certain as communities have changed. The city
can be home to people from a bewildering and stimulating variety of
cultural backgrounds and faiths. Urban Vision began its work in the
late 1960s among the Asian communities in towns still coming to
terms with significant communities from Pakistan, Bangladesh and
India. An ex-missionary from overseas speaking Urdu was judged to
be the ideal person for evangelistic outreach to recently arrived
Pakistani families. Now our mission partners meet British Asians
more comfortable speaking English, having careers in the profes-
sions and building their businesses. They may also in the course of a
few days deal with people from countries as diverse as Albania and
Afghanistan.

Slough has been transformed by new IT industries and huge
changes to its population. Well-educated Indians have been
recruited into these new industries. In addition to families of Indian
and Pakistani origin – Sikhs, Hindus, Muslims and Christians –
there are individuals and families from Iran, Iraq, Algeria, Somalia,
Sri Lanka, Nigeria, Zimbabwe and Romania. Urban Vision's
mission partner in Slough taught English classes, with many of these
cultures represented in one group.

Some people have a tenuous hold upon the territory they inhabit,
clinging to an inner-city bedsit or flat in need of repair, depending
upon job-seekers' allowance, existing off the black economy. Some
are asylum-seekers settled by the National Asylum Agency living a
hand-to-mouth existence on limited benefits. Such people can be a
shifting, rootless population, liable to be moved on, likely to slip out
of view, hanging in together in shared insecurity and adversity,
turned in upon themselves and upon people who share their nation-
ality, with few meeting points with the host community. Such
contacts they have tend to be with officialdom in its various guises,
or perhaps with a local community centre or refugee organization
providing support and advocacy.

Members of inner-city congregations need to take the initiative in getting to know who is on their street, making the first approach of friendship and offering to become family to those without. In Birmingham the churches have established a befriending project called Restore. It provides training for volunteers who then are put in touch with asylum-seekers to help them find their way around the agencies, support them through appeal hearings, find furniture for a flat, and simply to be a friend. The initial project has stimulated several other local church befriending projects.

Leeds Asian Ministry is a project set up by churches. In 2000 it was able to support creatively an opportunity provided by an Age Concern Millennium Award granted to an older person to organize English language classes for the under-25s. They reported in their first classes students from Mexico, China, Hong Kong, Poland, Ecuador and Korea, reflecting the overseas student population of Leeds. In addition LAM ran a home-based tuition service, reaching into 30 homes. Christians do more than teach English: they establish friendships, listen to people's problems and often provide reassurance from knowing someone in the host community with a strong religious faith.

It can be important to provide meeting points across generational and interest groups such as the Christmas party in Old Trafford, organized by Christians for the whole community, or their summer event in the park. Food, games, celebrations cross culture divides and help bind people together, so much so that some Muslims who tried to prevent their co-religionists from joining in were given short shrift. Cultural diversity is acknowledged and celebrated through cultural events that give dignity to people. Memory of homeland can be kept alive by encouraging people to tell their stories. Imaginative ministries will nurture the potential that people have to take some control over their lives and also to help others.

We must not forget that the inner city is home to white residents whose parents and grandparents lived, worked and died there. They have seen great changes with successive movements of incomers, East European Jews, Irish, Caribbean, Pakistanis, Indians, Sri Lankans and Bangladeshis. Each new group has to struggle for acceptance, and in proportion to their entrepreneurial skills and tenacity, move up the ladder. The changing corner shops, the worship centres, community organizations, multicultural schools, the less visible social structures and positions of influence in the neighbourhood tell the story.

In east London this process has continued into suburban Ilford. One Baptist church there is adjusting to its multicultural neighbourhood that includes the well-established South Asian communities and people of Kurdish, Iranian, Iraqi, Afghani and Albanian origins.

In Tooting, south-west London, a place my mother as a young woman knew as entirely white, there are nine well-established Asian churches or fellowships: three predominantly Sri Lankan, two Pakistani, one each of Mauritian, Filipino, Punjabi Indian, and Singaporean origin. Issues facing these churches are that none have their own premises, their leaders are largely self-financed through their own work, they are sometimes supporting members with ongoing asylum and immigration applications, and they are largely apart from mainstream churches.

These Christians feel and understand what it is to be on the margins of society. They know all about unemployment and social injustice, but lack the training and resources to tackle them. Our role is to give Christians the confidence to discover and use their own gifts together with God's resources, and help them realize the unity God has given his people. Community research, training, advocacy and action for social justice are beginning to emerge from this input.

But how is Christian witness to be made when another faith community is strongly entrenched in an area? I was introduced to the Ghamkol Sharif Mosque in Birmingham, which is reputed to have the largest worship hall in Europe. Every Friday it has several congregations to accommodate all who want to pray. Along the street on both sides it has bought up properties in which to establish a training and employment project, education classes, a funeral business, offices and a building company. The building company has renovated the properties and given a uniform Islamic appearance to the exteriors. In Southall, what is claimed to be the largest Sikh gurdwara outside India dwarfs the local Anglican church and puts pressure upon its activities through sheer force of numbers of worshippers using surrounding streets.

These are very obvious statements about the ownership of these urban areas. Whose territory is it? Does the Christian Church have the right to engage in evangelism there? If there should be a Christian presence, what form might it take? Sharp questions for Christian presence or mission are posed. Adaptability, risk-taking, a radical kingdom theology and an intuitive grasp of the Holy Spirit's ways seem to be needed for ministry and mission in multifaith, multicultural Britain today.

———————————

An Incomer's Tale

Mark Perrott

Director of the Regeneration Trust, working to redress poverty and
promote community in the World's End Estate, Chelsea, and Tollington
Park, London. The Trust also runs the School of Urban Mission

A lesson from John

Skinhead, short, fat and angry; John shared his dad's interest in law
and order. His dad a police officer; John one of those keeping his dad
employed! But it was John who first brought into focus for me the
challenge that faces the largely white middle-class Church in the UK.
Our home town was prosperous, with plenty of churches catering
for the prosperous community. But as one of a group of late teens
from a Presbyterian church, I began to question why folk from the
local estates seldom darkened the door of our church.

We could not reconcile the fact that while God loved all equally,
and Jesus died to offer new life to all, the Church seemed only
accessible to a particular, albeit sizeable, group – who shared a
certain level of education, wealth and networks of relationships.
Well-intentioned and enthusiastic (very naïve), we set up a ministry
to the skinheads and punks.

Having taken a group camping in the Mourne Mountains, John
said, 'But Mark, we can't come to your church.' 'Why's that, John?'
His answer was simple: 'Because we don't have the clothes you have
to wear to come to church.'

There is much talk today about social exclusion. One of the questions we need to face is, 'Who is doing the excluding?' If we are
honest, we may find that the Church is part of the problem.

Church or project

In 1988, I got involved in the Earl's Court Project, a joint venture
between Youth With A Mission and Holy Trinity, Brompton. Earl's
Court had major issues with homelessness, addictions, prostitution,
HIV. Here, the working/middle-class analysis was too simplistic. The
issues were those of pain and struggle, not traditional 'class issues'. It
did not take long to see that while expressions of street evangelism
and compassion had value, the 'missing ingredient' issue was the

need for Church – a community of people to belong to where people could begin to find healing and restoration. If we were going to encourage people to leave their life of prostitution, were we really offering a better, stronger community that they could belong to instead, caring for one another, protecting one another? Although people in need pray prayers of commitment, this meets more of a need in those 'doing'. It is symptomatic of a profoundly dualistic 'soul saving' theology that fails to reflect the full humanity of Christ.[1]

At the end of a summer outreach in 1998, there were about ten people who had made some profession of faith, but there seemed little commitment to their discipleship. So we set up a group meeting in a basement flat in Earl's Court. The group included a middle-aged alcoholic, two men struggling with paranoid schizophrenia, one transsexual and another young guy selling himself for sex.

Little by little we saw God's Spirit at work, reassuring them of the Father's love, encouraging them to make him part of the struggles they faced. Some months later, the members of the group went their own separate ways. Later we established a Fellowship in Earl's Court where we began to see more people from the street scene, at one point with four rent boys (male prostitutes) in our home group.

It left us convinced that a missiology without an appropriate ecclesiology completely missed the point. With hindsight, I think it is wise to have a few more 'healthy' people, to carry the 'wounded'. Like the story in Mark 2, we must become what John Ortberg[2] calls 'a community of roof crashers', reasonably healthy people together willing to carry those 'paralysed' to Jesus.

New beginning at World's End

Ministry in Earl's Court is like trying to build a church on a railway platform – everyone is always coming and going. Given its transient nature, we began to look at what we could do to have a more lasting effect. We found that many of those wheeling and dealing in the area, young women living in the YWCA, grew up on the World's End Estate, a mile away, in the poor (less celebrated) side of Chelsea.

Having researched and prayed for some time, with the agreement of the local residents' association and with encouragement from the local borough, we established a Community Church on the estate in 1997. The estate had been betrayed by the established Church, with the only church building (purpose built) on the estate closed and rented to an outside organization. We secured a disused studio on the estate, at the base of a 17-storey tower block. That room, once renovated, provided a base to start building a new church community – Homework Club, women's 'Pop-In', English tuition for Bangladeshi mums, worship service. A charity, The Regeneration Trust, enabled us to begin grappling with what community ministry and being Church might look like in such an area.

The key challenge for my wife and me was that this was to be Church for our three daughters. Despite our concerns, they thrived, and learned to love and minister to children their own age and younger who had seen a lot more pain in life than they had. They became more compassionate and loved the fact that since the church was small (about 30 people) everyone knew everyone by name.

We felt we had no right to come into the area and 'preach' to people. Alongside prayer-walking round the area (often in pouring rain) we began serving the local community. The first open door came through The Besom Foundation,[3] who had a request from Social Services for someone to help decorate a flat for a widow suffering from manic depression who spoke little English. We got to know the lady and her three teenagers, who were key drug dealers on the estate. Since then, things have grown to include a Computer Training Centre, serving about 800 people each week, counselling for women who have been abused, support and training for single parents, and a growing youth work. We are currently exploring what we can do to express God's Jubilee heart by helping those who struggle with debt.

Why $B^4 = I^2$

Recently, we have explored the *Belonging, Believing, Behaving* model. We may go one step further by beginning with *Blessing*. This is what Robert Lewis[4] calls the Church of Irresistible Influence: I^2. Let's serve unconditionally, take a *RISK* (a *Random Incidence of Spontaneous Kindness*),[5] give visual aids of Grace, provide some 'living proof' that we can use words to explain. Let's build a place, a group, a new community to belong to as part of the journey for those coming to believe. This is one of the strengths of *Alpha*[6] (something we have done with the homeless, the addicted, in pubs and council flats) as it allows people to belong while they find out more about following Jesus. The hope is that changed behaviour and lifestyle will follow.

Probably the greatest challenge is in the Belonging part of the equation. It is perhaps the challenge to our comfort zone that is the main issue for those of us coming from a more privileged background than those for whom the struggle just to keep going, to survive, is their day-to-day experience.[7]

Notes

1 G. Tomlin, *The Provocative Church* (SPCK, 2002, p. 105 ff.).
2 J. Ortberg, *Everybody's Normal Till You Get to Know Them* (Zondervan, 2003, p. 49).
3 The Besom Foundation is a Christian charity based in South London. It helps people make a difference. It provides a bridge between those who want to give money, time, skills or things, and those who are in need. It ensures that what is given is used effectively. The service it provides is free: www.besom.com/
4 R. Lewis, *The Church of Irresistible Influence* (Zondervan, 2002). A very helpful book that tracks the journey of one large evangelical church towards a more holistic understanding of mission and its relation to the local community.
5 RISK (Random Incidence of Spontaneous Kindness): a term used by Youth With a Mission.
6 For more details on the Alpha Course visit http://alphacourse.org/
7 Ann Morisy's book, *Beyond the Good Samaritan* (Mowbray, 1997), is a very helpful resource on community ministry alongside those who struggle.

Searching for Roots: Power and Powerlessness

Richard Springer

Director of the OK Club, a children's and youth centre in South Kilburn, London

> I don't feel no ways tired
> I've come too far from where I started from
> Nobody told me, that the road would be easy
> I don't believe He's brought me this far to leave me.
> (Revd James Cleveland)[1]

They arrived on the back of tidings that here in England there was room for them. The long-standing dreams of Afro-Caribbean blacks (and other immigrant groups) swinging onto these shores dressed up to the nines, fresh haircuts, and summer dresses, cultivate an image of embarrassing naïveté for those that have followed to deal with. The road was never going to be easy.

The last 50 years has been messy for Afro-Caribbeans in Britain (not discounting other communities or those that have been here for much longer), but in its response to various adversities I feel proud. Post-war British history tells us that immigrant communities' reaction to racism and other prejudices was often quick, organized and successful. Blacks developed the 'pardoner' system: pooling resources together to buy property. The Asian community organized politically, protesting through the Indian Workers' Association and the legendary Grunwick strike in London, which lasted ten months. These were corporate reactions to the frosty welcome from the host nation and came under scrutiny in the press and parliament who soon cast immigrant communities as a growing troublesome threat, a paranoia which reached its height infamously in Enoch Powell's 'Rivers of Blood' speech in 1968; countering an unpredictable but always biased system of prejudiced curriculum, lack of gainful employment and poor housing is tiresome toil.

Black Pentecostalism comforted the weary soul, offering a place of sanctuary, a place in which to wail. This welcome refuge from the cold world outside – including the established 'white' churches – gave birth to a generation. Second-generation black Christians are still coming to terms with their identity in this distinctive and complex community.

A whole host of things is at work here. Despite the admirable stubbornness of the post-war arrivals, they were voiceless. These immigrants needed to find a medium for articulating their woes. The Church provided a platform, a sense of ownership, some power. Physically the Church still carries the noise of pain and freedom; nothing beats the spontaneity and energy of a black congregation in worshipful unison. Now there was a captive audience for the ministers, a Church in a deep valley; for this first generation their sons and daughters.

The experience of those who arrived here as small children and British people of migrant descent is quite different. Biblical language is no longer suitable. The rural terminology of hills and valleys does not belong in the urban experience. New watchwords are constantly evolving, but power and powerlessness best describe the seeming difficulties of the relationship between the Church, the host culture and young black Britons.

So where now is this generation's place in Britain? The militancy and riots of the 1970s and 1980s challenging police authority and government has long since faded as an option for belonging to a coherent movement, and as a group, young to middle-aged black people are struggling to make their mark on Britain. There is a new awkwardness as the community fumbles around, dabbling in middle-class sensibilities, or sells its soul to the streets where today the illegal drug trade industry dominates. As the Israelites of the Bible tumbled from one catastrophe to another, creating a love–hate relationship with God, second-generation black Britons are, in clusters, gathering around the Church's periphery. Some have re-entered, and there is something of a black Pentecostal renaissance.

Where I live in north-west London the New Testament Church of God churches are brimming with confidence and people. The old schoolers remain, but these churches count that elusive 20–40-something crowd as members. One could say that this type of thing has happened from time to time during church history; among ourselves we call it revival.

The prodigal sons (and daughters) are returning, but not necessarily in shamefaced despair. Congregational expression still evokes emotion like no other Western worship, but the terms of engagement have changed. The Church must be more than a refuge where we express ourselves, relieved to be free. Our theology must also relate God to the outside world where we forge new roles daily. The perception is that the Church of our fathers was yet another response to the environment in which it found itself; the difference being, in those rented church halls they had the voice, the power. All week these men performed menial tasks way below their competence, but on a Sunday their churches developed a dependency on the elders as omnipotent characters while looking longingly to the hills from the valley.

The way of the Afro-American church phenomenon is well documented and is now courted, particularly in London, among second-generation independents. Some of the similarities are so uncanny one can only conclude they have been copied. Perhaps this is more groping in the dark? If it feels awkward, it certainly does not look or act awkward. After all, this is Church, the outworking of a group's journey with Jesus Christ. There will always be transition in relationship.

The head-scratching perplexity of finding identity while swinging on the pendulum between power and powerlessness or stretched on the continuum of certainty and doubt is where God meets people. The dangers of declaring one more vital than the other have claimed victims within the black Church and beyond, and the press have had a field day.

The black Church gave birth in transition, producing a restless child. Perhaps our response to future awkwardness will be to engage with the arising uncertainty. If we fail to ask and grapple with questions, surely we run out of things to say?

Note

1 'I don't feel no ways tired' reproduced by permission of Malaco Records.

Recent Arrivals

Wagih Abdelmassih
Pastor of the London Arabic Evangelical Church, London, and Director of Agape Arabic Christian Centre

In recent years, immigrants have increasingly come to Britain seeking better economic and living conditions. Large cities such as London receive a huge number of asylum-seekers. The majority of them are not prepared for the change. They are in need of language teaching and social advice.

Therefore it is normal for new immigrants to feel lost and lonely, and the Church could play a big part in overcoming those problems. I am the pastor of the London Arabic Evangelical Church and Director of Agape Arabic Christian Centre; my church comes across quite a few of these people, from different faiths and racial backgrounds. I will give you one example.

A family converted from Islam to Christianity. Back home the father was jailed for nearly a year and the whole family persecuted for more than nine years. They were under different kinds of persecution, from their government as well as their relatives. They were pushed out of their own house, and they rented flats instead. They moved to seven flats in two years because the government followed them everywhere they went. One of the two children was kidnapped, and it was not easy to get him back. Some Islamic groups tried to kill the man's wife and their children.

So they asked for help to move from their home country. They sought asylum at the British embassy but the immigration authorities in the United Kingdom refused to accept them. They arrived in London after a lot of difficulties with the British embassy as well as the local authorities in their country. They got through it with the help of the London Arabic Evangelical Church, West London Baptist Churches and the Jubilee human rights campaign. At last they arrived in London to face a completely different culture and society, where they needed to have a local church backing and supporting them.

That was one of the stories, in brief. It raises some points that the Church needs to be aware of.

Immigration issues

- Recent arrivals need immigration and social advice.
- Quite a few serious asylum cases are not accepted as refugees in the West because other untrue or false cases prejudice officials against the genuine ones.
- Members of other groups often suspect that where some get jobs in the immigration or advice offices, they favour their own ethnic group over others.
- Christian and Muslim immigrants and refugees often feel they are in conflict over access to official services. Christian refugees fleeing persecution in Muslim countries are frequently shocked to find Muslim officials in charge of helping their case.
- An advocate is needed. We have a family in our church, who have lived in a bed and breakfast for more than a year, because they have no one to act as an advocate for them when attending these offices.
- The immigration and social authorities have recently given responsibility for refugee cases to the National Asylum Support Service and Refugees Arrivals Projects, and many mistakes have since happened.

Social needs

- Recent arrivals feel strange in this new society. They are vulnerable, seeking to relate, but afraid to be cheated. The Church must offer them a sense of trust and belonging. The Church's responsibility is to understand the new arrivals' cultures.
- Education, especially language teaching, is very much needed. Many of the recent arrivals need advice on occupational, educational, family and religious issues.
- The Church can help in finding jobs or connecting people with employment agencies.
- Through in-depth interviews with some of the recent arrivals, the Church can find out why they are here in the community. Then it will be clear what their need is and what the Church can do for them.
- It would be good if the Church could afford to provide hostels in the local community for some people or be in contact with housing authorities. That would help to solve the biggest problem which new immigrants face.
- English language classes are very helpful to adult new immigrants in London. If the Church can offer some classes free of charge, it would be a good witness.
- Most are in need of computer courses and to be trained to cope with the new lifestyle.

Evangelism

- The Church must do evangelism, without any contradiction or compromising. It is not forcing anyone to believe, but marketing the gospel effectively.
- Some churches give their buildings for use by other religions. These churches are trying to be generous, thinking they are building a bridge of 'love'. Unfortunately some of the other religions or cultures only see this as a sign of weakness to be taken advantage of.
- The message of grace is the best communication tool to the diverse mix of culture and languages.
- In the case of Muslim converts the Church has to be aware that some ask to change their religion for immigration reasons only. Some think it will help their case. The Church may have to delay

their baptism until they make sure of their situation, and not quickly give them a document supporting their case before making sure of their faith.

Finally, there is a real need for the Church to be involved in racial justice ministry in an urban area like London. This will help to overcome the difficulties newcomers face. One way to do this is by building an International Church involving both English and various immigrant congregations. We are trying to do this in west London.

Questions for Further Thought and Action

1 (a) Find out what those from different faith communities in your area believe and how they express their identities alongside others in the UK today.
   (b) What is their vision for Britain in the future? Are there any areas of common concern on which you can co-operate?

2 In partnership with other local congregations, explore how together a joint project might be developed to minister alongside some who are socially excluded in your area.

3 (a) If you have moved to the city from elsewhere, think about what the experience has taught you about the Christian faith and its expression. How does this relate to your experience and participation in 'Church'?
   (b) If your family migrated to the UK, what have been the issues and concerns which have guided you in negotiating the cultural and faith issues of belonging or not belonging?

4 Identify and link up with those civic authorities and voluntary bodies which deal with those newly arrived in your community. How might your church best provide for their basic human rights and needs?

8

Peace-making

We have given this title to the chapter because it is a positive flip-side to the more usual, but negative, 'conflict-resolution'!

Christians typically avoid conflict, but there are some occasions where conflict is a necessary step forward toward realizing the kingdom. Challenging injustice, healing hurts, reconciling disagreements all depend on facing up squarely to conflict.

There are some conflicts which are particular to urban living. Others share in wider cultural divisions – of race and religion. Yet other conflicts are unfortunately peculiar to the special practices of the saints themselves, as we stumble toward Jerusalem!

Patton Taylor writes from Northern Ireland a long-view story of change amidst political troubles and population changes. He shows how religiously motivated outreach has developed from evangelism to intentional community development.

Geoff Reid describes the response of the churches to the rise of the far-right British National Party in northern England. He demonstrates the need for rapid-response Christian action to keep up with a quickly advancing political landscape. His story also illustrates how essential it is for Christians to take an overtly political stand even (or especially) when it entails taking risks.

Paul Keeble tells a personal story of how he became involved in a project addressing the increasing culture of gun crime and gang violence in the inner city. He shows how both believers and unbelievers in a neighbourhood can combine to deal with crucial issues.

Tim Foley examines the role of mediation in the local congregation. The presence of so many hurt and wounded people in our churches, together with the stresses generated by the situation we find ourselves in, gives rise to many conflicts in our churches. Some of these are over big principles, many over personality clashes. Either can cause untold damage to a given faith community. Tim shows how a process of mediation can help resolve disagreements.

The 174 Story

Patton Taylor

Principal and Old Testament Professor, Union Theological College, Belfast

It had been a long night. The coffee-bar outreach of the previous evening had gone well enough. The music group had been given a good hearing. Round the tables the young people who had come in from the New Lodge community were asking penetrating questions of the outreach team members – and there was a real searching for spiritual reality. However, an uneasy air of tension hung over the hall. For this was in the early 1980s, at the height of the Northern Ireland 'troubles', in the midst of one of the most disturbed Catholic-Nationalist districts in the city. Recent political events had led to major riot scenes; and that evening there was an uneasy stand-off between the angry young men on the streets and the nervous police and army patrols.

Suddenly the door of the hall burst open. 'The Brits are coming,' someone shouted. Within moments the hall had emptied and a full-scale riot was under way in the lower Antrim Road outside.

This Summer Outreach was an annual event based at Duncairn Presbyterian and Antrim Road Baptist Churches. A team of young people, mostly students, would gather for two weeks for Holiday Bible Club and coffee-bar activities – in the midst of this deprived urban community torn apart by sectarian strife.

Both churches had been built 120 years before amid the orchards and gardens of a fashionable new suburb of the city. Now that same district was 'inner city' – with all the deprivation common to most contemporary UK inner-city communities. Until the early 1970s, the community had been 'mixed', Protestants and Roman Catholics living together. But most of the Protestants had fled to the suburbs because of the 'troubles'. Duncairn and Antrim Road churches now found themselves in the heart of an almost entirely Catholic and Republican community.

The next morning the team gathered to plan the activities of the day. Could the nightly coffee bars continue among riots and disturbances? A local girl on the team broke into the discussion. 'You've got it all wrong,' she said. 'You think that the barriers between you and these kids are because of politics and because of the Protestant–Catholic thing. But these kids don't really care about any of that. *The real barrier between you and the kids is that you're all so middle class and affluent.* You come in from outside and you don't know what it's like to live around here.'

That comment led to the founding in 1983 of the 174 Trust – a centre for evangelical witness and community action in the New Lodge district of Belfast. We had come to realize that the main problems of our district were typical of those of any UK inner city. Yes, they were overlaid by the politics and 'troubles' of Northern Ireland. But the underlying issues of poverty and deprivation were the same. We realized that, instead of a team parachuting in for a 'hit and run' raid of evangelism each summer, we needed Christians permanently living in the community. I was already living with my family in the Duncairn Manse, and we began a small residential community of young folk nearby. We realized our ministry was to the whole person: we had to do something to tackle social and community need, not just preach at people! So an employment action scheme, a mums' and toddlers' group, a pensioners' club and a community café (the Saltshaker) emerged, as well as youth work. Mary Malanaphy, the first director, lived above the café and was 'on call' round the clock.

The name '174 Trust' came from the address of the project at 174 Antrim Road. The original logo, in which the numbers 174 overlapped to form two crosses, also resembled the cross-roads where the centre was situated – the themes of the cross at the centre, cross-roads and decision, taking up a cross, the cross representing suffering and deprivation, the cross as a bridge across Northern Ireland's sectarian divide.

The early years saw several young people coming to faith. However, there were also numerous setbacks. Billy[1] was shot dead by the army in his early twenties. His parents told us that 174 was the only place he had found stability in a life marred by struggle and violence. Sean in his late teens had all the appearance of faith, and wrote moving Christian songs and poems. Tragically he lapsed back into street violence and is now serving a life sentence. Mary's new-found faith met with great resistance among her family, and contact with 174 was forbidden. We never did achieve our early aim of planting a local community church in the district.

There were the perennial questions of the balance between social action and evangelism. Family pressures made it difficult for us to maintain the original vision of all staff living locally. There was the issue of contact with the local Roman Catholic parish – indifferent rather than antagonistic to our work. How were we to avoid the assumption that to become a Christian must involve becoming (in Northern Ireland terms) a 'Protestant'?

Another issue was contact with paramilitary groups. Because we were a Christian group, we were largely immune to interference from 'the Provos' – but we knew such immunity could disappear if they felt we had overstepped the mark in drawing young people away from the paramilitary cause. Could we have any witness to the paramilitary leadership? We learned our real enemies were not the paramilitaries, but 'the principalities and powers in heavenly places'.

There were discussions over the extent to which 174 should remain an evangelical organization or should work in partnership with others. Our conclusion was that we should remain a group of evangelicals seeking, under God, to make our distinctive contribution to the New Lodge community, but not claiming that we were the only people through whom God was working, and committed, without compromise on essentials, to working in partnership.

Church members too had to make a paradigm shift. Duncairn congregation realized the time had come for them to move. A new worship centre was built some distance away for the traditional membership; and the old church, halls and manse were made over to the 174 Trust for community ministry. This enabled a big expansion of 174's work. At that time (1994) I moved away to take up a theological college teaching post (from the coal face to the cloister!).

In more recent years, the emphasis at 174 has changed. In the early days, 174 was the only thriving social action project in that district. Today community groups and projects abound. Many traditional indices of poverty no longer apply. The focus at 174 has moved to community development, to do things *with* people rather than *for* them – to empower local people to run their own community facilities.

We have learned that *paradoxically we have more influence now that we have less control*. Our desire to share the gospel is undiminished; but staff now do so primarily by working alongside local people and taking opportunities to share their faith informally.

The present director of the Trust, the Revd Bill Shaw, a Presbyterian minister, is highly thought of in the New Lodge community and throughout the Catholic-Nationalist communities of North Belfast.

Because he has the confidence of the Catholic-Nationalist community, he has also had opportunities for involvement in 'peacemaking'. He was instrumental in the recent conflict over Holy Cross School (which made world news).

We believe God has led us along the community development road in which it is the living out of 'kingdom values' that gives us the opportunity to speak of the eternal Good News.

Note

1 The names mentioned in this section have all been changed.

Race in Northern Towns:
Christian Responses to BNP–Muslim Tensions

Geoff Reid
Methodist Minister and Team Leader at Touchstone Centre, Bradford

If ever a project was set up to respond to a race riot and a rise in the number of BNP candidates at the local elections, it must be Touchstone. We are an agency of urban mission specializing in city political/social issues and interfaith work.

Following the Bradford disturbances of 7 July 2001 we came in on Monday morning and cleared our diaries for the next three weeks as we set about helping the churches cope with what had been described as the worst race riots on mainland Britain for 20 years. I use 'churches' in a fully ecumenical sense because over the past 14 years this Methodist project has steadily come to be regarded as a resource for all the mainstream churches in Bradford.

At the (technically illegal) anti-BNP rally on the Saturday afternoon I warned the crowd in Centenary Square about racism in the national media which meant that any serious trouble would blight the city's reputation for years to come. By the evening I was talking with local residents on White Abbey Road with the Rector of Manningham, the Revd George Moffatt, as we watched the petrol bombs raining down on ranks of riot police.

Bradford duly received the bad publicity. However, having shared in the investigations of the Churches' Commission for Racial Justice working party on the 'Northern Disturbances', I am not convinced that we suffer from racism and its effects more than the other Pennine towns.

In the 2001 Census 75,188 residents of Bradford Metropolitan District declared themselves to be Muslims (16.1 per cent). This reflects a combined Pakistani/Bangladeshi population of 72,961 (15.6 per cent), most of the remainder having Indian backgrounds. Meanwhile in 2001 the National Front/BNP presence in Bradford was minuscule. The ostensible immediate cause of the disturbance on 7 July was the threat of a BNP march taking place. This had actually been banned – like the Saturday afternoon rally arranged by the Anti-Nazi League and the Bradford TUC. The tiny group of neo-fascists ('laughing into their pints') had the pleasure of seeing the city burning, whereas all they had to do was start a rumour. The underlying causes are complex, but Dr Philip Lewis is surely right when he describes sections of a generation of young Pakistani males as 'double orphans', alienated from both mosque culture and white society.[1]

However, it was Oldham that produced a BNP General Election result of 16 per cent in its two seats and Burnley which elected three BNP councillors in 2002 and another five in 2003.

Since the late 1990s Touchstone has produced for local churches a simple A5 anti-BNP leaflet *Love Casts Out Fear*,[2] which has gone through various versions. It invites people to 'overcome despair with confidence in Christ' and gives a theological basis to celebrating diversity and unmasking the racism of the BNP. This is followed by a brief update of BNP activities locally, and a prayer.

This was the only resource we provided on the subject until the election of West Yorkshire's first BNP councillor in Halifax in March 2003. It was clear that the party were going to make a big push for seats across the county. The spur to do something more about the BNP actually came from the Revd Lisa Quarmby, the Methodist minister in Illingworth Moor, Halifax. She was seeking advice after receiving a leaflet from the local BNP candidate which referred to his own past and his family's present involvement with the Methodist Church in his leaflet.

After consulting with another minister in Bradford, I suggested the following form of words to the Halifax Methodist Circuit staff, which formed the basis of a letter to newspapers and was subsequently read out from the pulpits on Palm Sunday.

> We were disturbed to see a leaflet in which past involvement with Illingworth Moor Methodist Church is used to solicit support by a BNP election candidate. The Methodist Church is open to all in its worship, fellowship and service to the community. However, we need to make it crystal clear that we reject the British National Party's policies and practices as incompatible with the Methodist Church's social teaching and our understanding of the love of God for all people.
>
> It is important that the people of Halifax make it clear that they reject the BNP and its attempts to stir up racial hatred and fear of asylum-seekers. This is a party whose activists encourage violence and several of their leaders have criminal convictions. The Methodist Church never encourages people to vote for any one political party. The distinctive nature of the BNP gives us good reason to urge people not to vote for it. In the coming council elections we urge people (i) to vote and (ii) to vote for one of the other democratic political parties.

These words were distributed to all clergy in Bradford wards which had a BNP candidate. The Bishop of Bradford met with Anglican vicars in these wards the following week. The Roman Catholic Diocese sent it to parish clergy outside Bradford.

In the event the BNP won Illingworth by 56 votes. In Bradford their eight unsuccessful candidates in wards close to Halifax and in Liberal Democrats dominated north-east Bradford scored between 16 per cent and 30 per cent. Nevertheless, in both Halifax and Bradford we believe that we took the right stance while the issues of race and asylum need more public debate. There is, of course, a constant dilemma in dealing with the BNP. Do we, in effect, give them free publicity or do we take a more restrained approach with literature purely for use with the churches? To provide an adequate response we need to do our homework and make clear the theological basis for our implacable opposition to this party's policies and ways of working, while trying to be both flexible and swift on our feet. In Bradford this means trusting one Christian organization to take the lead and do the spadework.

Notes

1 *The Tablet*, 21 July 2001.
2 Available from admin@touchstone-bradford.org.uk or in hard copy on receipt of a stamped addressed envelope at Touchstone, 32 Merton Road, Bradford BD7 1RE.

Gang Violence

Paul Keeble

Director of Urban Presence, a project resourcing inner-city churches and Christians in Manchester

It could be said our awakening to the growing problem of gang-related violence in Manchester was a literal one – thanks to the searchlight of the police helicopter at 3 a.m. as two armed suspects were caught in our back yard! As long-time residents raising a family in the Longsight area of Manchester, two fatal shootings near our house raised our concern further.

Gun crime has plagued the Moss Side, Hulme and, more recently, Longsight areas of inner-city Manchester for a number of years. Statistics like 13 dead in a three-year period, plus woundings and hundreds of incidents involving firearms, tell only part of the story.

In June 2002 local people organized the 'GangStop' march. The turnout, the positive press and media coverage, and the fact that a number of the organizers seemed to be members of local churches, was all encouraging.

But having a march to say 'No more!' is relatively easy; attempting to identify and solve the problems of which street-crime, drug-dealing, gangs and violence are the symptoms is another matter. To address this, a number of community meetings took place after the march which the Revd Les Isaac was invited to facilitate. Les, himself an ex-gang member in London who had helped inspire the march organizers, asked me to get in touch with church leaders I knew, locally and across the city, to encourage them with their members to support the community meetings and subsequent events. We also organized two further meetings specifically to envision church leaders.

'The only time people listen to me is when I point a gun at them.' These words were said by a young man during the rally after the march. Bravely speaking on behalf of the gangs, he said that there are reasons why gangs attract young people and that we needed to understand and to listen, not just lock them up. At the community meetings the attraction of gangs came up again and questions were asked such as: 'Why are young people creating their own alternatives?', 'What is missing from our communities and from our family life?' (I could add 'church life'), 'What messages are young people getting that make them feel left out?', 'Where are the fathers and positive role models?', 'Why are police eight times more likely to stop and search a black young person than a white one?', 'Why are so many failing in (or being failed by) education and employment?' Gangs provide them with identity, a 'buzz', excitement, a group to belong to, and the means to acquire money to get the things our society tells them – and us – they 'had to have'.

It is a short step from questions like these to words like 'discrimination', 'exclusion', 'racism', 'materialism', 'poverty', 'injustice'. Are Christians equipped to deal with these issues biblically? What came through at the community meetings was an invitation for churches to get involved in the process. One comment was: 'Where are the Pastors?' It seemed the people were more aware of a role for the Church than the Church itself was! This openness to the Church represents an opportunity for practical expression of God's love. If our gospel has nothing to say about these issues, then we might as well stay within our buildings and ignore the world.

A few of us agreed to form a community-based organization to ensure 'life-chances for young people in the community'. This became 'Carisma' (Community Alliance for Renewal, Inner-South Manchester Area) and was launched in November 2002 at a community meeting where local people were elected to join the Carisma Core Group. The ethos is to work positively for and on behalf of young people, as created and valued by God to see them given viable opportunities to fulfil their God-given potential. It is not a Christian organization as such, but most of us involved are local Christians, and those who would not describe themselves as such are sympathetic and share the values.

Too often 'young people' are seen as a problem. Is it not more the case that young people have problems, many of which are rooted in the failure of the adults that are supposed to give them guidance, affirmation and role models? Of course there is also a bit of human nature – the lure of easy money.

Carisma will not necessarily create these life-chances. Rather we see a need to identify what is going on from a local standpoint, assess how well it is being accessed and how effective it is being; to build on strengths and plug gaps. A lot of money has been pumped in already in an effort to solve the problems, and there is also a need to better network the many existing organizations and to represent the community's views to them – especially the statutory ones. One-third of our Core Group are under 25.

We also want to maintain the public profile started by the march, and keep the agenda of peace in people's awareness. So in February 2003 we held a 'Peace Week'. We organized and ran two local events called 'Generating Peace' at which local people were invited to sing, dance, rap, act, recite poems etc. on the theme of peace, and a Memorial Service in Manchester Cathedral for those who had lost loved ones to gang-related violence. We also invited local churches and schools to put on events during the week, and contacted some local businesses for sponsorship.

The 'Generating Peace' events were great fun but with a serious message, and a reminder of how talented folk round here are. The Memorial Service was powerful and moving, with around 500 local people along with civic dignitaries. My one disappointment was the almost complete absence of church leaders from outside our immediate area, despite a number of appeals.

Individual local church members have been involved and support-ive right back to the march, but the leader is the key to pulling a church behind an initiative like this. Why do some church leaders choose not to get involved? In some cases a dualist spirituality puts 'evangelism' on one side of a sacred/secular divide and 'social action' on the other.

Others are caught up in the machinery of running their churches and unable to extricate themselves to take on anything more. 'Urban ministry fatigue' may also play a part. For leaders of churches outside of the area this is quite clearly an 'SEP' (Someone Else's Problem).

We have had spoken encouragements and eloquent, passionate-sounding prayers offered up, but little in terms of visible, practical support. People round here vote with their feet and so judge the support of others quite simply – by whether they turn up or not!

The challenge for the churches in community involvement is to have the flexibility to grasp opportunities that come along and get involved.

Rather than being manufactured by the Church (or any other agency), the desire for peace in the community, tapped into and channelled by a few individuals (who happened to be members of local churches), provided the impetus. Hence there is local owner-ship – 'bottom-up' rather than 'top-down' – and more chance of being something that truly serves local people. God is at work in all sorts of ways that we are unaware of. Pray for openings and oppor-tunities to join in, but make sure when that prayer is answered you are ready to take them!

In the Congregation

Tim Foley

Mennonite pastor with the Green Field Community Church in Portadown, Northern Ireland. He works with church, with young people and with reconciliation initiatives

I urge Euodia and I urge Syntyche to be of the same mind in the Lord. Yes, and I ask you also, my loyal companion, help these women. (Philippians 4.2)

At the heart of the cross is Christ's stance of not letting the other remain an enemy and of creating space in himself for the offender to come in. (Miroslav Volf)[1]

In truth, we must say that the church has too often failed the world by its failure to witness in our own life the kind of conflict necessary to be a community of peace. (Stanley Hauerwas)[2]

The conflict in High Street Community Church focused on Frank, the part-time youth worker. The budget meeting was coming up and funds were tight. Frank badly wanted the congregation to invest in a video-editing suite so that the youth could use film to explore the Bible and attract local youth. Anticipating resistance, he began to phone sympathetic church members and got several people on his side. He then e-mailed the whole congregation, urging them to invest in the youth rather than waste money on new hymn books and carpet for the building. Soon, church members and families were taking sides – defending Frank or attacking him. The pastor and other leaders tried to avoid the conflict but began to feel insecure and threatened as the conflict escalated. It was a tense budget meeting that gathered the following week. Most people wanted to tackle the issue and vote on Frank's proposal before discussing Frank's behaviour.

However, a wise church member requested that the discussion be postponed and a process designed to help the congregation deal with the issues. She suggested the formation of a small group composed of her and one representative from each side of the conflict. Two weeks later the group recommended that an outside mediator be invited to come alongside and walk the congregation through a conflict transformation process. They pointed out that conflict had erupted a few times in recent years and that the congregation needed to learn the skills to deal with it. After some lively discussion the congregation accepted this, and a mediator was carefully appointed a month later. After gathering information about the conflict the mediator began by training the congregation in basic conflict skills and facilitated a healing process to help restore relationships.

The mediator helped Frank to recognize that his behaviour was divisive and coached him in a healthy decision-making process. He apologized for the hurt he had caused but was also affirmed by most of the congregation in his role. The leaders were shown how to face rather than avoid conflict and to stay emotionally connected but not submerged. Crucially, they began to learn how to define themselves in a clear and positive way and to take responsibility for their own spiritual nurture. It turned out that everyone wanted the youth to have the best resources possible – but some wanted to buy more of Frank's time rather than new equipment. Finally it was agreed that money would be made available for renting rather than buying equipment and that Frank would be paid a further half-day per week. This was a win–win solution for most people. One family decided to leave, but a leaving party was organized and blessing given on both sides.

Congregations can be reluctant to invite a mediator to help transform conflict because they view conflict as un-Christian, opt for quick win/lose solutions and resist the complexities and energy required to problem-solve. But because conflict is inevitable, there will be times when help is needed from the outside – a neutral and safe intervention. At risk is the future health of the congregation and its witness in the community. Mediation provides a way to deal constructively with conflict situations. It is a voluntary process that is fair and respects people who cannot find a way through on their own. It helps people transform conflict from something destructive into something life-giving.

Richard Blackburn[3] outlines the different phases in conflict transformation. In the *Information-Gathering Phase* the mediator learns as much as possible about the conflict by reading minutes, interviewing or using questionnaires. The *Education Phase* introduces training for the whole congregation and coaching for key people. Here the basics of conflict transformation are taught and conflict in the Bible examined. The *Healing Phase* involves group dialogue in order to help people let go of past hurts and move towards forgiveness. Mutual confession rather than blame is the idea. Active listening is a crucial skill that can radically improve the atmosphere around a conflict. This involves putting one's agenda on hold, inviting the other to speak, summarizing, and waiting for the right time to reply. Translating 'You' into 'I' statements (e.g. 'I feel angry' rather than 'You make me angry') is another important skill. The *Problem-Solving Phase* documents the diversity of interests in the congregation along with brainstorming and evaluation of any proposals. The purpose is to come up with creative agreements between the parties. A key goal in mediation is to get behind positions to interests. A position is a demand framed as a solution (e.g. 'We must have video equipment now'). An interest is what lies behind a position – needs, hopes, concerns (e.g. 'The nurture of our youth is important to me'). It is vital that these be distinguished and interests addressed. The *Closing Phase* involves a written report that summarizes the whole process and details specific agreements reached. A time of worship then helps to bring closure and a sense of hope and newness for the future. The emphasis throughout is on process rather than outcome. If the process is trusted, the outcome can be trusted. The idea is that the congregation will learn how to transform conflict for itself.

The congregation should have teaching about the role of conflict in Scripture. In Acts 6 the Church redefined priorities and put in place new structures in response to a conflict over the needs of a minority group. In Acts 15 the Church was a forum for listening, discernment and prophetic direction alongside clear leadership (and conflict prepared the way for new revelation – Gentiles do not have to become Jews to join God's people). 1 Corinthians 6 and Philippians 4 show that mediators have been necessary from the early days of the Church. We learn in Matthew 5 that unresolved conflict gets in the way of our relationship with God and that we should initiate reconciliation. Matthew 18.15 f. shows that conflict is a normal part of congregational life, that we should move towards conflict, that God is present in conflict and that the goal is reconciliation.

The congregation that prepares for conflict will experience less destructive conflict in the long term. The congregation that tries to avoid conflict will probably suffer. This is the paradox: to have less (destructive) conflict we need to have more (healthy) conflict. This is why conflict can divide and weaken one congregation but unite and strengthen another. Congregations can discover that conflict can be transformed into a creative life-giving process that strengthens relationships and energizes people for following Jesus. The good news is that we can have conflict without destroying one another.

Note

1 Judith Gundry-Volf and Miroslav Volf, *A Spacious Heart* (Trinity Press International, 1997).
2 *Christian Existence Today* (Baker Books, 1995), p. 95.
3 In Carolyn Schrock-Shenk and Lawrence Ressler, *Making Peace with Conflict* (Herald Press, 1999).

Questions for Further Thought and Action

1 What are the sources of conflict in your neighbourhood? How can your church, in partnership with others, develop reconciliation ministries in these circumstances?

2 Who is involved in active peace-making in your locality? How might your church best support these people and initiatives?

3 Who are the socially excluded and disaffected young people in your area? Where are they? How might bridges be built to them? By whom? How could your church play a part in developing inclusive projects?

4 What are the causes of conflict in your congregation? How is this expressed? Perhaps it is suppressed or hidden? How is this dealt with and by whom? In what way can this be improved?

9

Some Other Urban Issues

It is difficult to limit the number of urban 'issues' once you get going. On what basis do we close the list? There is no end to the specialist ministries that are needed to address the multiplicity of needs we face in our neighbourhoods.

We could include children's ministry, youth work, family centres, women, sex workers, men's groups, homeless people, etc. Here we have picked out just four. Some responses seek to work constructively with local and national government programmes; others express a prophetic rejection of government oppression.

Simon Standen illustrates how a local church can work with government policies on healthy living to address a wide range of community needs, and create openings to proclaim the gospel.

Bob Holman, on the other hand, criticizes government policies on debt for actually making the predicament of the poorest families worse. Christians may try to ameliorate some of the effects of government policy on the poor, but should not delude themselves that they are thereby fundamentally altering the situation.

Terry Jones shows how a local church can combine spiritual vision and practical savvy to set up practical projects from the institutional church base to provide training and employment for people, using its resources of people and property.

Dave Rogers, on the same issue of employment, demonstrates a different approach. He illustrates how Christians can work within government programmes to help individuals find work.

A Healthy Living Project in a Local Church

Simon Standen

Church outreach worker at Ilford High Road Baptist Church, London,
seconded from Interserve's Urban Vision

How does healthy living relate to the work of the local church?

At Ilford High Road Baptist Church we asked this question in 1998 with an extensive survey into the needs of the local multiethnic community. As a result a separate charitable company, Healthy Living Projects, was formed, which became responsible for all the church's existing community-based activities as well as developing new initiatives. The aim of Healthy Living Projects is to provide holistic care for the people living in the neighbourhood of the church.

Our history

Our church was founded over 200 years ago and has been very active in the community. It has a very good reputation, particularly with its work among children through the Pre-School which has been running for about 25 years, and Young Inspirations which is an after-school club. In 1996 a Family Contact Centre was set up, where the absent parents of families who are separated can enjoy contact with their children in a safe and neutral environment. In 1996 Language Link was formed, aimed at providing English classes for ladies.

The church finished the refurbishment of one of its buildings in 2001 and opened the Welcome Project. As a first step the Welcome Project aims to meet the needs of the vulnerable and isolated. Many of these are refugees, asylum-seekers and homeless who live on the street, in cheap bed and breakfast or poor quality housing. The project provides free washing facilities, hot meals, nurse, chiropodist, hairdresser and an information and advice service.

All the projects are very much interlinked with people often using several together. It is also very clear that the ethos behind all the projects is Christian; however, the ways in which this is expressed is always appropriate to the circumstances. The project seeks to meet immediate need first, no strings attached, and witness flows from service. Many meaningful relationships have been cemented over lunch.

Take for example Mbarime from Albania, who first attended Language Link in September 2000, but then, following a period of illness, became very depressed. Mbarime and her husband Ilir were among the first clients of the Welcome Centre. Slowly through various volunteers in the centre befriending this family, they decided to come to church. Following a series of Bible studies Ilir gave his life to Jesus in December 2001. As Mbarime saw the change in Ilir she too began Bible studies and became a Christian in May 2002. She says, 'Since coming to the Welcome Centre my life has really changed. I have come to church and now my life has changed 100 per cent. I am no longer depressed and so I can also look after my husband and children.' Her youngest daughter has really enjoyed being a part of the pre-school project for the last year.

Another lady from Kosovo who attends the Welcome Project came to England four years ago, having lost many loved ones in the Kosovo war. Eight months ago she started attending the Mother and Toddler group and now says, 'I came to the group because I felt alone, I needed to make friends and be with people. Now I have got many friends. I discuss with them my problems and concerns. I can spend two or three hours just talking.'

It is not just adults who benefit from the Welcome Project. Children are always welcome and during school holidays the Centre can be very busy. One ten-year-old who saw and even experienced much violence in Kosovo says, 'The Centre makes me very happy because I can meet and play with other children who have similar backgrounds.'

The Welcome Project deals with all sorts of people, including some homeless men. One of these, Mr Singh, had been banned from the gurdwaras for his drinking habit. The Welcome Project was able to help him, and he often attended church although he sometimes heckled the preacher! When he was seriously injured in a fire the only contact he would give was the co-ordinator of the Welcome Project as he said, 'That's my home!' This man was really searching for something in his life and certainly heard the gospel clearly, but we don't know if he ever made a commitment: he died from TB earlier this year.

English classes

Language Link is very much aimed at Asian ladies who for a number of reasons do not feel able to attend English classes in college. A number of ladies started attending Language Link because it was convenient while their children were in pre-school. Gradually they gained confidence in their abilities in a relaxed environment. Some have since gone on to college to gain qualifications, while others have been able to gain employment.

Then there are a number of ladies who have lived in England for 20 to 30 years and have never really learnt the language. Now that their children are grown up they want to learn, but find that their families often ridicule them for their attempts. These ladies gain a lot of confidence in the classes and usually realize that they can communicate far more than they originally thought. One Pakistani lady met a Somali lady in the local park and they talked for two hours. The Pakistani lady was so excited when she came to class the following week that she just kept on saying, 'I can speak English. She understood me. I am not stupid!'

As we come into contact with various people in the community we are able to contribute to their 'health' in many ways. It may be in the practical provision of childcare or a hot meal. It may be through listening to their problems and being a friend. It might be through the building of self-confidence as a result of learning the language. For some it has been through a life-changing experience of being introduced to Jesus.

Debt

Bob Holman
Works for FARE (Family Action in Rogerfield and Easterhouse) in Glasgow

The New Labour government, to its credit, introduced a minimum wage, the working families' tax credit, increased benefits and a host of area initiatives. But people who live in deprived areas know that poverty remains. The evidence is the enormous amount of debt among those on low incomes. On the Easterhouse estate, where I live, the local Citizens Advice Bureau dealt with 2,501 cases of debt in 2000–2001. In Britain, hundreds of thousands of citizens are so poor that they have to borrow to survive.

The problem of debt is a theme in the Bible. Small farmers who struggled in times of drought and other disasters had to turn to unscrupulous lenders whose high interest rates were difficult to repay. The lenders then took people's clothes and even their children. Years later, Jesus told stories which featured debt (for examples see Matthew 18.23–35 and Luke 7.41–3). His emphasis was that lenders should forgo debts with the implication that God would forgive their debts to him.

Today Christians should be concerned to tackle the evil of debt for the reasons found in the Bible. The reasons are that debt oppresses poor people beyond measure, that the impoverishment of debtors fragments society, and that the gains made by lenders feed the sin of greed.

The Social Fund

Within contemporary Britain, the evil of debt can be illustrated in three directions. First, in debt to the government. Before 1988, people dependent long-term upon welfare benefits were entitled to replace essential domestic items like fires, cookers and furniture. At that date, the Conservative government implemented legislation which replaced most grants by discretionary Social Fund loans which are repaid by automatic deductions from incomes.

Social Fund recipients found themselves repaying between £5 and £35 a week, from what was already considered a minimal income. The results were devastating. Research revealed that 70 per cent of those repaying loans experienced difficulties in affording fuel and clothes.[1] In opposition, the Labour Party promised a return to grants. Once in power, it refused to take action. The outcome is that over a million and a half people still have loans. I know a lone mother who, after repaying a Social Fund loan, buying food, toiletries, cleaning materials, paying for fuel and heat, the TV rental and the children's fares, has 30p left a week. She has to be a better keeper of a budget than Gordon Brown. Nonetheless, when an unexpected demand happens, like a child needing new shoes, she has to cut down on food for herself and try to buy a second-hand pair.

Loan sharks

Second, legal loan sharks. In 1998–99, 689,000 applications for Social Fund loans were refused. Others do not qualify for the government system. Where do these needy citizens turn for credit? Not to the low-interest services of banks and building societies who consider that around 7.9 million applicants are so poor as to be a bad risk. So, many take high-interest loans from certain shops. The shops target the poor with slogans like 'No deposit and no credit checks'. Families desperate for furniture sign up and get immediate delivery, but the costs are high. For instance, a sofa bunk at a cash price of £432.38 works out with interest added for weekly payments to £777.38. Some find that they cannot maintain payments and lose the goods.

Then there are the doorstep firms. These companies offer instant vouchers or cheques. Poor people are tempted to obtain consumer goods, with a particularly high take-up rate for Christmas presents for children. But the loans have to be repaid, with typical high APR being 164 per cent. The outcome is absolute poverty for the debtors. Yet there is money in poverty. In 2001, one company made pre-tax profits of £169 million.

Third, illegal loan sharks. A young father stole my wallet. Later he showed me his knee smashed by the shark's baseball bat. He had borrowed for food and clothes for his children. When he fell behind in repayments, he got a beating. He stole to avoid another one. These criminals offer instant money, no questions, no forms. The interest rates may be 500 per cent, enforced by violence.

A response

The locally run project with which I am associated has a small hardship fund. The bed of a child of a lone mother collapsed. Her application for a Social Fund loan was refused because she was repaying an existing loan. She would have turned to a shark but the hardship fund was used to make her a grant of £220. The project's committee is not entirely happy about the hardship fund as it means it becomes a conveyor of charity which judges who should and who should not get the goodies. But it has to do something.

The project's premises are also used by a credit union, which is a better way of helping in that participants are partners, not just recipients. Credit unions are non-profit-making organizations in which members have to save for several months before they can obtain a loan which is limited to two and a half times their savings. Repayments are at a rate not more than 12.6 per cent. The credit union to which I belong has over 600 members and nearly all loans are repaid. Loans are not for thousands of pounds but for a few hundred which, for instance, enables the purchase of a cooker without paying enormous interest rates. The drawback is that credit unions reach the poor but not the poorest, who cannot save even a small amount. Notably, a number of credit unions are based in churches.

Churches have also been prominent in the Debt on Our Doorstep Campaign under the umbrella of Church Action on Poverty. It has lobbied, often in conjunction with people who are themselves in debt, to persuade the government to replace Social Fund loans by grants: so far without success. It has also made the case for legislation to follow the example of other European countries by putting a cap on consumer credit rates. The depressing response of New Labour has been that it does not wish to intervene in the workings of the market.

The real cause of debt is that many people have incomes, whether from earnings or benefits, which are too low. Such poverty is unacceptable in a society where some families can spend more on one meal than others receive in a week. This is God's world and Christians should be making the case that both excessive wealth and excessive poverty are inconsistent with Christianity.

Note

1 M. Huby and G. Dix, *Evaluating the Social Fund* (DSS, 1992).

Work: Toxteth Tabernacle Baptist Church/ Toxteth Vine Project

Terry Jones
Pastor at Toxteth Tabernacle Baptist Church, Liverpool

'Work'

'If you don't see, what you don't see, you'll never see it!' It took me a few minutes to grasp this dynamic statement of faith, followed by the realization that it was a perfect commentary on Hebrews 11.1:

'To have faith is to be sure of the things we hope for, to be certain of the things we cannot see' (GNB).

In 1989 I looked out on a vast Victorian edifice: largely unmaintained, semi-derelict and riddled with rot. A monstrosity requiring instant demolition! Everything I hated – it shouted; 'God is irrelevant', an ancient and archaic relic to be dismissed and derided. 'Please keep out', was the statement of the angle-iron fencing and forbidding rows of steps. The only redeeming feature was the absence of 'This is the gate of heaven' over the entrance arch! Yet try as we might, and we did to the point of architect's drawings, the new church building failed to materialize. Two specific words from visiting ladies to a Sunday service forced us to roll up the plans, pay off the architect and apologize to the rather bemused congregation. 'I can see one of those huge cranes with the demolition ball at the end, and it's coming towards the Tab.' In perfect harmony two people blurted out, 'What happened?' The reply, 'It missed!' The second contribution sealed, or saved, the day, 'I believe there is a word for you; God says, "Take your hands off the building and I will show you in due time what I will do."' We humbly obeyed.

Within six months I was beginning to 'see what I could not see'. An emerging vision, borne out of information, visitation and prayer, that would redeem the building for church and community. A step-by-step 'pattern of building' (Exodus 25.9) that would take us on a roller-coaster ride of faith, vision, partnership and almost unbelievable financial supply.

Step 1 was *information* that would lead to *identity* with specific need, and then *involvement*. Over the years the church had almost completely lost touch with its local community. Small pockets of compassion, service and love remained, but it was known as the 'posh' church that no longer lived on the streets or fully understood the struggle and stress of Toxteth life. We desperately needed new bridges of love that would help to restore good relationships, change the community's perception of God – and us – and allow us access points for the gospel. Every step we took was precipitated in the community, either through the result of surveys, the consistent visitation of every local amenity or by word of mouth from the street. Combined with that 'local' knowledge was the prayer, vision, faith and commitment of a small band of believers. Hopelessly without resource, yet 'seeing what we could not see'.

'Tab' Pre-School

Step 2, and a massive leap of faith, was the establishing of a Play-group, later to become an Ofsted-registered Pre-School catering for 26 two- to four-year-olds each day, five paid staff and a willing band of volunteers. We received 100 per cent in our first Ofsted inspection and have had a waiting list of around 20 for the past 12 years! Many local people have been trained for work, with a number gaining NVQ 1–3 during their time with us. Children, impossible to place elsewhere, have been accommodated, including one who had 'come to die' with a life expectancy of months. Twelve years ago his mum asked me to do his funeral. I met her some time ago and reminded her that 'I'm still waiting!'

Stepping stones

Step 3 was the transformation of a typical 'Victorian' church lounge, with its many shades of brown, into a modern restaurant. An 'oasis of peace' amidst the stress of much urban life. Ten years on, it is packed with locals, dominated, on occasions, by working men and far more 'church than church!' Here, much of the urban communication takes place: pragmatic, raw and often rough! Yet it is a place of salvation where some have found Christ, received prayer and stepped out of the stranglehold of drug dependency and despair. Local people have found full-time work, trainees have matured, and otherwise unemployable people have found a place of service. It is a thrilling place in which to express our faith in word and deed.

Level 3: 'Education Otherwise' provider

Step 4 was the transformation of 3,000 square feet of very derelict basement into a highly professional, high-tech and much respected school for excluded and disaffected 14- to 16-year-old students. After numerous battles for recognition it is today a full partner in 'Education Otherwise' provision with a curriculum to be envied by others that includes information technology, pottery, design technology, textiles, domestic science and a full programme of literacy, numeracy and personal development. Awards have come steadily and with them respect, multiple funding packages and a pioneering zeal that is both preventative in practice for those 'at risk' but presently in school, and deeply committed to bringing hope and a future for those for whom Level 3 is their last education opportunity. Reality is also faced. Many don't last, but for some who do the future has brought full-time employment, further education and the lasting knowledge that they were loved and valued during their stay in the school.

In spite of a membership of 58 the Lord has continued to add staff with faith-defying regularity: a Children's and Family Worker, Missionary to Muslims, Charity Development Officer, Tab/Tear Fund Worker allied to an amazing team of volunteers who work tirelessly in Kids' Clubs, local schools, Club-culture and all the normal activities of a living church.

These 'bridges of love' have utterly transformed the community's perception of who we are and given us many opportunities to speak of Jesus, share his compassion, fight for justice and serve our city. The windows that once went through on a weekly basis no longer need protective wiring. The robberies, theft and vandalism so endemic in the first six years have largely given way to respect, ownership and genuine acceptance of our place at the heart of the community.

The rebuilding agenda, in all its dimensions, has a long way to go, but we rejoice in every evidence of God's gracious blessing and we press on 'to see yet more of what we presently do not see'.

Employment

Dave Rogers
Chief Officer of Hull Council for Voluntary Service

My story begins with the kind of person many will have met in urban ministry. He was a young man in his early twenties, with a drug habit which he was trying hard to control, with a partner with whom he had a small child. He had been out of work for most of his working life and had no qualifications and very little experience – nothing much to trade with in the jobs market. There are many people like him in Hull. Wanting to do the best for his family and be able to afford a few presents as Christmas was approaching, he took a temporary job through an agency. They set him to work, cleaning in an abattoir. His job was to clean up all the blood and scraps of bone and meat on the floor where the animals were slaughtered. He was paid a very low wage (before the days of the Minimum Wage), and no protective clothing was provided. He was expected to provide his own overall and boots. He came home at the end of the day covered in filth.

After a few days he complained about the working conditions, saying his chest was getting bad from breathing in the rubbish in the atmosphere. He asked for a face mask to be provided. Shortly after that, he was told he would not be required any more at this job. Then he developed a fever and other symptoms and was taken into hospital where he remained throughout Christmas. Not only was he not able to provide the special Christmas he wanted for his daughter, his family ended up visiting him in hospital.

Fortunately he recovered from this incident, after being seriously ill for some days. But this story, and others like it, highlighted for me the question of whether the Church can do anything to help situations like this. I want to tell the story of two ways in which the Church was able to help.

I had been commissioned by the Church to a ministry as an Industrial Chaplain in Hull, in particular to make relationships with the statutory and voluntary sectors, and to work on issues of the local economy and urban regeneration. As part of this ministry I had become involved with Hull Council for Voluntary Service and was then the Chair of its Trustees. In 1997 we were approached by the Department for Employment to see if we would be interested in delivering the Voluntary Sector option of the new Labour government's New Deal Programme for young unemployed people. We had to do a good deal of heart-searching about this. We had seen and experienced the previous government's Project Work programme, which had appeared to exploit young people as cheap labour and to exploit the good will of the sector while offering very few real opportunities for employment. We commissioned a couple of public meetings for voluntary organizations where the issue was fiercely debated, and eventually decided to give it a go. It was hard work dealing with a contracting process with a government department, but there did seem to be a genuine desire to let us experiment and be flexible in the way it was delivered. We could see that there were shortcomings in New Deal, not least that it only offered the benefit rate plus a few pounds, and that it was still short term, lasting only six months. And initially it only applied to 18- to 24-year-olds. However, it was far better than anything that had gone before.

After the first year of delivery we commissioned some independent research among the young people who had gone through the programme. As a result of their feedback we decided to develop our own enhanced version of New Deal, based on the Intermediate Labour Market model. Intermediate Labour Markets are a way of offering people a real job, paying them a proper wage, rather than benefits, for a limited period, combined with skills-based training and development, and intensive help with job-finding and the necessary skills for that. We managed to put together a package of funding, including monies from the New Deal programme, together with European Social Fund and some Single Regeneration Budget money controlled by the new Regional Development Agency. Our hope initially was to offer this as a two-year job for those who needed it. In the event, about 15 months was the maximum we managed. But this approach proved to be highly successful. While other government programmes were achieving something like 30 per cent of people going into jobs, our Intermediate Labour Market achieved between 70 per cent and 80 per cent.

Why is this important as an example of urban ministry? Theologically speaking, we could talk about the evil of unemployment, how it destroys lives, taking away hope from people, making them physically and mentally ill, and so on. All of this is proven and researched and documented. And therefore by being involved, the Church is offering a ministry of hope and healing in a very practical way, after the example of Jesus. It seems absolutely crucial to me that the Church was prepared to allow my time to be used in this way, to give itself, without asking for any return, without asking 'What's in it for us?'

However, there was something in it too, because churches, although they are often unaware of it, are part of the voluntary and community sector. There is an increasing awareness that we can, as churches, take advantage of many things on offer from the statutory sector without necessarily letting that control our agenda or dull our prophetic edge. Churches were able to engage with our programme by providing work placements for people on New Deal and the Intermediate Labour Market. What they received were often very committed people, wanting to get into jobs and so anxious to learn new skills and play a part in whatever church project they were placed. As a result they often made a significant contribution as workers in those projects. Churches were able to give a supportive environment where people could grow and learn, enhance their skills and be given confidence.

One young woman came to work in a local church community centre where there was a range of child-care opportunities, including a Parents and Toddlers group, two-mornings-a-week nursery, and an after-school club. She had achieved a qualification in child care from the local college and was excellent with children. She had not been able to get a job for two years, because she lacked confidence in herself and went to pieces in interviews. After six months' placement with the church, she was able to enter paid employment. Here was the Church, in a very practical way, helping to overcome barriers to employment, and to bring someone the hope, dignity and self-respect which comes from being able to do a job, earn a living and contribute to the common good.

Questions for Further Thought and Action

1 How might your church contribute to the health and well-being of your neighbourhood? Think about setting up a project. Are there other agencies you could consider working alongside?

2 Can you discover the extent of debt in your community and church? In what ways might you minister to this need? Could debt counselling or a local credit union contribute to the well-being of your community and provide a means of ministry for your church?

3 Do an audit of how and how much your church premises are being used. Consider how the church plant, property and facilities could be used to benefit people in the area.

4 Contact your civic authorities and explore with them how your church could be involved in enabling unemployed people to obtain the necessary skills to enter the job market.

10

Faith-sharing

Among many urban practitioners 'evangelism' is a dirty word. Too often it has been an excuse for middle-class Christians to assuage their guilt at the expense of inner-city people. Too often it has amounted to little more than wordy preaching without any practical care.

The separation of evangelism and social action, however, has contributed to the numerical decline of many inner-city churches, and the closure of their buildings. We need a recovery of evangelism which is an integral part of a missiology that combines demonstration and proclamation. While some sectors of the Church have been guilty of talking too much, others have spoken too little. They have been good at loving in the name of Jesus, but not at naming the name of Jesus; not at giving a reason for why they are doing what they do, or passing on the faith which they enjoy, in the One whom they love.

Derek Purnell gives us an overview of a holistic urban strategy, based on his own experience in ministry on estates. He emphasizes how theory must be rooted in action.

Amanda Gray shares her experience in the sensitive area of evangelism among those of other faiths. She shows how we must love before we speak, and how our speaking must avoid both expressing the prejudices of racism and provoking the understandable suspicions of the community.

Howard Astin writes about a new development in church life that is fundamentally evangelistic – cells. He demonstrates that cell church is relevant to the inner city and is not simply a middle-class phenomenon. Instead it provides opportunities for genuine relationships and the exercise of leadership among church members, as well as supplying a space for relational evangelism.

Finally, **Juliet Kilpin** describes her experience of church planting. Frequently church-planting strategies have resulted in middle-class clones of existing churches. Juliet argues that we need new approaches to birth new forms of Church that are authentically part of the inner-city environment rather than being imposed upon it.

Urban Mission

Derek Purnell

Co-Director of Urban Presence, a project resourcing urban mission in Manchester

My understanding of urban mission was formed from my background, experience and study. I will describe them briefly and then offer some reflections.

Background

Growing up in an unchurched working-class family on an outer housing estate in Birmingham was significant; I have always been conscious of my roots. Similarly, coming to faith in a church plant that was particularly successful evangelistically has influenced my perspectives.

Local church experience

The small inner-city church in Manchester that grew while I ministered was effective in mission not because of any exceptional techniques, personnel or unique projects. Most of what was done was very ordinary. On reflection, the positive aspects of church life were: it was highly relational, visual, tenacious and pragmatic. The character of mission practised in the church was 'Wholistic' and 'Saturational'. We attempted to minister to the whole community in as many contexts and ways that we could. Any evangelism that was exercised appears to have only been effective because of the other aspects of ministry to the community. Evangelism tended to be house-to-house visitation, children's missions and various events. Occasionally we'd do something mad, like pub evangelism. Prayer was foundational to all our activities and ranged from prayer weeks and prayer walks to regular weekly prayer times for leaders and members.

We were active in the community with a presence in various community groups and the governing body of the local school, and were often in the local newspaper for a variety of reasons, from campaigning to sponsored events. The church maintained a real presence in the community through family sports days, fun days, barn dances, bonfire nights, praise marches, and in local park events.

All ages were represented in the church and catered for: infant blessings, children's choir, youth club (and football team), men's badminton and also seniors' events.

The projects were small and related to those with whom we had contact, including an unemployed club, parents and toddlers, homeless house, Jubilee ministry (decorating and gardening). Social action was mainly in response to need and ranged from responding to practical need to helping those with addictions.

Research

The research that I later conducted, 'Rediscovering Effective Principles for Urban Church Models and Mission with Particular Reference to Manchester City Mission 1837–1914' revealed that MCM in the 1800s was particularly effective because it was relevant, contextual, wholistic and exercised a ministry wherever its clientele were to be found. I was surprised to find similarities in what I had been involved with, as much as I discovered other principles. It reinforced that it is not just what we do (models of urban mission) or how we do it (methodology) but also the underlying principles and how we engage (attitude) with those with whom we wish to minister.

Reflections on urban mission

I have become increasingly troubled with the concept that *everything* we do is 'mission'. It is true that there is a sense that *anything* we do, if it is truly *Christian,* is 'mission'. There are also those who would suggest that only when we are engaged in social action are we truly engaged in mission. However, not all social action is 'Christian mission'. When social action is no different in character from secular social work or a humanitarian response to human need, it can hardly be termed 'mission'. It must in some sense be Christian and reveal Christ.

Finding and revealing Christ in the city

There is a real concern regarding urban mission that we come to the city to bring Christ, failing to see that he is already there. If we fail to understand the challenge of Matthew 25.34–45 we will fail to see Christ in the city because the most destitute is made in the image of

God. However, we must also take care that we do not deify human suffering; suffering of itself is no 'blessing'. Blessing only occurs in the way we deal with or respond to suffering, otherwise it would be better to leave the suffering in their misery to be blessed by it. What a perverse philosophy that is! We can always be challenged by and learn from those who are suffering, but if we bring nothing we have no mission. Although Christ is already present in the city, this is rarely perceived; while we may debate whether we bring Christ, we certainly should reveal him.

Good works and our salvation

There is a sense in which good works affirm our own salvation, which is by grace through faith, for Christ is manifest in active Christian love. What I am saying is, I am only truly fulfilled when I am doing what I am created for: serving God in proclamation, good works or worship. These are not options – they are a package and are dependent on each other. As Christ is manifest in active Christian love, so the power of the Holy Spirit is evident in the prophetic announcement of shalom. The Old Testament often defines worship in relationship to righteousness and justice. It is hardly surprising that Jesus states that '. . . those who worship him must worship in spirit and truth'.

Sacred space or sanctifying presence

We should take note that Jesus does not focus on place with regard to worship but on the person. We need to pay attention to this and not be led to pursue some mystical concept of sacred space or place. God does not dwell in buildings. He did not spare his temple or Jerusalem for the sake of his people. Those who need to take sanctuary should be able to find that in the people of God. Buildings are often a great resource as long as they are not the objects of our attention or places that we hide in and that screen God's people from the world. Our concern should be to be a sanctifying presence as Christ is with us and we take his peace with us into the world. That peace; that shalom; that wholeness; that sense of well-being, is what needs to be communicated in word and action to the city.

Mission that results in transformation

The Scriptures from Moses to Jesus demonstrate a liberating faith, and Paul teaches and engages in a mission that demands transformed lives – no one is to stay the same. This is radical, not civilizing or Christianizing, mission. Orthodoxy that does not result in orthopraxis and transformation is probably only a cerebral faith and not a wholistic one, which is evident in the Bible. If there is no transformation, we have nothing. It is this radicalism of the City Missions and Salvation Army that made them so effective – it is raw, gritty, uncomfortable and cannot be ignored by society, Church or State; it is only ever popular with the people to whom it ministers.

Church and mission

The Church should be the kingdom's greatest expression of mission, but it must move on from meaningless symbolism in the established Church, unintelligible hype in the newer churches and mediocre blandness from everything in between! We need to be demonstrating the thoughtful, vibrant, challenging and confident Christianity that is visible in the Scriptures!

Evangelism in a Multifaith Setting

Amanda Gray
Local Centre Co-ordinator for Interserve's Urban Vision

The setting

Our Centre is in a predominantly Muslim inner-city area of a major northern city. The local population is very mixed, being made up of Bangladeshis, Pakistanis, Yemenis, Somalis, Afghans, Kurds, Iraqis, Iranians, Libyans, Syrians, Malaysian students and families. Some have been in the UK for 30 years, some are newly arrived. Some speak fluent English with a local accent, some none at all, despite having been here years. Non-Muslims consist of some Zimbabwean asylum-seekers, some of whom are Christians, and some white people who are mainly elderly. Most younger white people have moved to the outskirts of the area or to the surrounding areas, probably as they have become a bit better off.

There are seven churches in this area of the city but all at one end of the area away from where most of the ethnic minority groups live. Churches at our end closed down as Asians moved in and they lost their clientele. Some of the churches aren't interested in the ethnic communities at all, two are liberal, with church leaders having bought into the pluralistic world-view, and the others see themselves as the remnant, believing that they have been pushed out of their own community. The Church has failed to engage with the Muslim population (though there is some awareness), and there is fear bred from lack of personal relationship.

The Centre

The Centre is run by a small local interdenominational charity which has been in existence for over 20 years, its purpose to reach out to local Muslims. Historically an individual or couple sought to make links within the community and to raise awareness in the city about reaching out to Muslims. My predecessor realized a lot of Christians had had their awareness raised but either didn't meet any Muslims or did so in passing, and little in the form of relationship was established. He conceived of the idea of a Centre, which eventually opened on 15 September 2001 (shortly after 9/11), a time that we felt was very significant. I began work as the Centre Co-ordinator the day the Centre opened, having previously worked overseas in Muslim countries.

Day to day

We function as a private community Centre, asking the community what they would like us to do and aiming to respond if we can. To begin, we engaged with women through teaching English, sewing, swimming, cooking, sauna and ice-skating. There have been many requests for keep-fit, which we can't fulfil. Now we have a girls' club, our idea but well received. Most Muslim children and young people attend school then mosque school, and we wanted to provide other input. We also do football, English and computers for men. We don't concern ourselves with numbers attending. Often it is easier to have conversations when there are fewer people there.

Reaching out

We seem to have favour with the wider community. We haven't directly engaged with the mosques, but they know we are here. We don't do any overt evangelism. If we did, people wouldn't come: the wider community would prevent them. Therefore I haven't named the Centre nor the city in which we work. If people ask, we tell them that we are Christians and that the Centre was opened to bring Muslims and Christians together in a place of peace, as historically there has been a lot of hostility and misunderstanding between the two groups. Barriers have to be broken down; misunderstandings corrected and trust established. Only then are Muslims likely to be open to hear about our faith. Most Muslims believe all white people are Christian and equate Christianity with all things Western, all they see on TV and video, believing that Christians believe in sex before marriage.

With the women, relationships are progressing naturally with many pre-evangelistic conversations taking place, offering to pray for people and getting involved in their lives off the premises. Most women come with felt needs of loneliness, boredom, rejection and fear. They talk freely about their religion and we are becoming freer from our 'normal' English constraints of not talking about ours.

Reaching men

Men didn't come naturally to the Centre. Those who work are often in the restaurant or taxi-driving business with down time between 2 a.m. and 4 a.m. They sleep until lunch and are quite busy until 4 p.m. when they go back to work. Asylum-seekers who are free have access to full-time courses. We have made one day 'Men's Day' in order to make it clear that the Centre isn't just for women. Segregation of the sexes is very important in Islam. This actually hasn't had much effect, and it looks like tutoring in men's homes (or maybe hanging out at the local snooker club) will be far more effective in bringing men together.

Families

We reach out to Muslim families. This might not seem unusual, but world-wide most converts from Islam to Christianity are young single men. We think and pray carefully about particular members of each family, knowing that mum comes to sewing, daughter to girls' club, father to English. It goes well beyond the nuclear family with many people within one ethnic group being part of the same extended family.

I think of the record-breaking domino attempts, where one domino is pushed, knocks into the next and so forth until each one falls down. We aim to influence *all* of the family, however extended, to develop an underlying sympathy which will lead to Muslims being able to follow Jesus and stay in their community. It is one thing to reach vulnerable asylum-seekers far from home and the constraints of their community, quite another to reach established, close-knit groups.

Volunteers

All volunteers are Christians, though perhaps local people will lead activities and Christians will attend (for example, Urdu or Arabic lessons, Asian cookery). Flexibility is important but within clear goals. Communicating those goals and equipping volunteers is my responsibility. Other challenges include: the need to break down barriers and misconceptions of local Christians, since most volunteers come from the middle-class suburbs, not locally; the lack of English language skills among 50 per cent of the people we meet; Asian youths into crime and drugs; a lack of vision for the lost by Christians.

Conclusion

Most of us grew up in a society where Christian values were the norm, so that as Christians we don't realize how radical our values are. Muslims comment, for example, that we do not show favouritism. To people who grew up in a system of currying favour and having unbelievable obligations to their relatives, not showing favouritism is tremendous. The Holy Spirit is at work in us and we shouldn't undervalue how different our lives are.

We have been open just over a year and a half, so it is early days. Personally I find it a spiritual battle as one and then another and another area of my life seems to come under the hammer. Satan is not going to sit back and let us just get on with reaching out to some of the most unreached peoples on earth. But the reverse of this is the realization that we may be weak and powerless, but God Almighty is our strength.

Urban Cell Church

Howard Astin
Vicar of St John's Church, Bowling, Bradford

In 1993 we decided to transition to become a cell church. We read about other churches' experiences and attended the International Cell Church Conference in Singapore: radical steps for an inner-city Bradford Church of England congregation.

The concept of cell church seemed to answer some of the issues that we faced. We wanted to see our membership mobilized so that the 20 per cent would no longer be doing 80 per cent of the work. In addition, we wanted a system that enabled our members' personal issues to be confronted and dealt with. Like many inner-city churches we had a membership with many problems. There were few professionals, few with further education, and many with life-controlling issues such as addiction and chronic health problems.

Would cell church work in this inner-city environment? I heard that cell church would work in America but not here. Others said it would not work in America, it was a Far Eastern concept. Others stated it was just for those cultures where there was revival. Nevertheless, we concluded that the Holy Spirit was using the cell church concept in different cultures and environments – in Mongolia, Russia, Australasia, Africa, South America, North America – but, in 1993, not in Europe. There were cell churches in big cities and rural areas – in towns, commuter belts and Urban Priority Areas.

We therefore ploughed on. For five years we kept quiet in case it didn't work! Only in the last six years have we gone public to show that in our environment, in Bradford, it works.

A changing culture?

There has been a change in our culture over these last 20 or 30 years. Although there was an emphasis in the 1970s and 1980s towards individualism, especially in 'Thatcher's Britain', now we see a desire for community and the deepening of relationships. This is a consequence of the break-up of family life and the resulting lack of security. In the secondary school where I am Chair of Governors, over 80 per cent of the pupils do not come from a family unit of father and mother. Either there are lone parents or step-parents, or guardians such as grandparents or foster parents. This is inner-city life. One of the consequences is a desire for relationship.

There is disillusionment with Church, yet people are still attracted to Jesus. Our British population has no less spiritual hunger, but they do not see Church as answering their spiritual needs. No longer in our urban setting would many people see the Church as relevant. How can we help people see that 'God is good and Christians are OK'?

As every church has its journey in its particular cultural setting, we must ask 'How do we do Church here?' In inner-city Bradford we need a way to provide quality pastoral care, including repentance and healing, while mobilizing the congregation to reach out as witnesses into the surrounding community.

In Bradford many inner-city churches have died or become small remnant congregations, with the membership living outside the city centre. Then there are the bigger eclectic congregations that gather from miles around rather than reflecting the inner-city community. God does not want us to desert our inner-city areas. But how can we maintain a vital presence?

Values

The values behind cell begin to answer these questions. Some churches have seen the way forward as being small groups. Yet if these groups do not own the values of pastoral care, healing and evangelism, they will not halt the decline of the Church within the urban setting.

Figure 10.1 shows the agenda of a cell group, with two foci – one inward and one outward. The inward focus is that group members build each other up and minister – including nurture, prayerful support and prayer ministry. Then the outward focus is evangelism and mission.

Vision statement

Once we had a vision statement that was so theologically correct it referred to each member of the Trinity – not even the vicar could remember it! We then believed God was telling us to keep it simple so we would all know what we are about at St John's. Our vision statement is 'To know God, to show God, and to share God'.

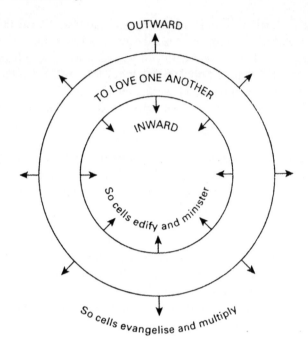

Figure 10.1: The agenda of the cell group

Our cell values

For us in inner-city Bradford, cell values are fivefold:

1 *Jesus at the centre.* We need him present in each cell meeting, we need him to show his way at the planning meeting, we need him in prayer ministry, we need his strategy for evangelism, we need to experience his heart for the lost, we need to know what action he wants us to take in our community

2 *Positive faith in God.* We have found this to be the antidote to the disappointment and disillusionment that tempt us away from our walk of faith (Philippians 4.6–7).

3 *Every-member ministry.* Ministry has many aspects – specific roles within cell life (praying for others, hospitality, leading, mission, intercession), our projects into the community (among the elderly, young families, youth, or those suffering from addiction).

4 *Caring community.* We have been slow to act as 'family' in cell. We slip back into the mentality of Church being a mid-week meeting and a celebration on Sunday. How often do we meet others from our cell outside these times? Do we share with each other things that concern us? Are we open to give and receive? Do we want to spend time with each other when there is 'no particular reason' to do so? In Bradford we have many peoples from different ethnic backgrounds and cultures. Should some renounce their previous religion and become Christians, this would mean for some that they would be ostracized from their family and culture. Would their cell satisfy their needs as a caring, loving community – 'family'?

5 *Living for the lost.* Each individual needs to experience God's heart for the lost.

My thoughts on ecclesiology and missiology have changed. For years, I saw the Church as having to work out its missiology. However, I am now aware that first comes missiology. This has been accentuated by living in an inner-city environment. We are sent out to make disciples, then we look for a form of Church to service that mission.

After the values – a different structure

The key to seeing the cells run effectively is to make sure there is good support and telling accountability for the leader. Figure 10.2 shows how the cells are arranged, with a co-ordinator being responsible for three or four cells. On a monthly basis the co-ordinator will visit each cell in turn and in effect monitor and evaluate its development, encouraging the leader in the delivery of quality pastoral care and effective mission.

So far – it works!

There are many vital areas of cell church life – the leadership training, the 'four Ws' structure to the meeting (welcome, worship, witness, word), the one-to-one mentoring, the '12½ Steps to Spiritual Health' course, and prayer.

The membership at St John's has been willing to investigate, learn, change and continually re-evaluate the effectiveness of what we do.

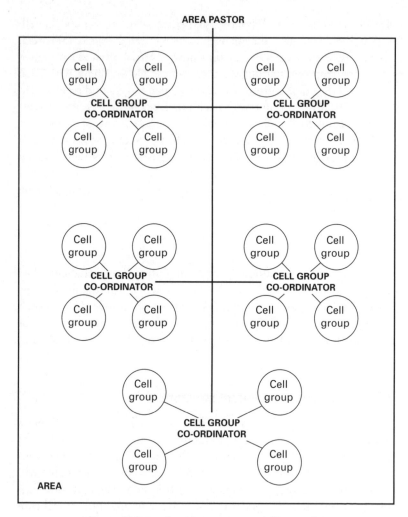

Figure 10.2: Leadership structure: working model

It is a thrill to see people from damaged backgrounds and messed-up lives experience the freedom that is there for them in Christ.

It is still our prayer that we continue to be used by God to see more people of inner-city Bradford join us in worshipping the God 'who is able to do immeasurably more than all we ask or imagine, according to his power that is at work within us' (Ephesians 3.20).

Church Planting

Juliet Kilpin
Director of Urban Expression and Pastor of Cable Street Community Church, Tower Hamlets, London

When I was a child attending church with my Christian neighbours, I was often asked what I wanted to be when I grew up. Apparently I regularly answered that I wished to be either a missionary or a minister. How these two job descriptions got separated I will never know, but here in east London I live a life where it is impossible to be one and not the other.

I live in Shadwell in Tower Hamlets, a community near the north side of the River Thames, between the City of London and the ever-increasing developments of Canary Wharf. It is a dense community, made up of numerous high- or low-rise blocks, with 30,000 people living in less than a square mile. Of our community, 65 per cent are first- and second-generation Bengalis, and the rest are mostly white working-class 'Eastenders'. Estimates suggest only 0.5 per cent of people here go to church.

I moved here in February 1998, after a long search for accommodation in an estate where most housing is owned by Tower Hamlets Borough Council. 'Why don't you ask the council for key worker accommodation?' I was asked. It takes at least five years to get a council flat here, and even then a one-bedroom flat is deemed adequate for a family of three. One Bengali family we know has 14 people living in a two-bedroom flat. No wonder the boys are on the streets all day, only returning late in the evening to pick up their sleeping bag and find a corner of the flat to sleep in.

During this painstaking journey two Christian agencies helped us. The Mayflower Centre in Canning Town gave temporary accommodation to me, my husband and our 12-month-old son. The Victoria Park Housing Association offered us shared ownership, enabling us to buy a maisonette in the locality.

But why Shadwell? My husband and I are Baptist ministers. Surely we could find a Baptist church to employ us and give us a manse. We came to Shadwell because we didn't think there would be many others who would want to! Urban Expression had recently started as an initiative to recruit church planting teams for under-churched areas of east London, and as the leaders of the first team we wanted to find those gaps. We saw this was a gap – yes, there were a couple of churches there, but we're talking about 30,000 people! The churches which witnessed faithfully here for centuries have seen many Christians leave the area, and many Christian projects try to 'save the East End' ('So you've come to "do" us have you?') and give up after two years because there was no 'fruit'. We wanted to come and work alongside these faithful beacons, learn from them, and contribute what we could to the task of seeking God's kingdom in this community.

Urban Expression grew out of frustration. The 'Decade of Evangelism' set targets to plant churches (one per 1,000 people – that means Shadwell needs 30!), but many plants had weaknesses. The most popular model was the mother/daughter. Although very successful, its weaknesses are: first, only churches big and healthy enough to lose a significant number of their congregation can manage this (which rules out most inner-city churches); second, because a daughter congregation is never planted far from the mother, churches are planted in well-churched areas; and third, most daughter churches look like their mothers. Which when trying to reach those who don't like church, never mind go, is a problem.

Urban Expression tries to break this mould by recruiting teams purposefully to move into under-churched areas and creatively consider how to be Church in that community. We moved here as part of a team of eight. As like-minded, passionate, mission-minded people we took a risk to try and create Church with and for the community. Urban Expression encourages experimentation, and therefore allows freedom to fail.

Being given a blank sheet of paper on which to design Church was daunting, and many hours were put into prayer, and discussions about doctrine, theology, ecclesiology and missiology. I will always remain grateful to those who helped lay the foundations of the work in Shadwell.

Out of these discussions came our mission statements: 'To discover and express the kingdom of God through being Church with the people of Shadwell', and 'To see households of believers on every estate in Shadwell'. There are some distinctive things about these, which express our foundational values.

We believe God is already at work in east London. He was before we arrived, and he will be after we leave. We haven't valiantly brought God into Shadwell riding on a white horse announcing the salvation of the East End! Our job as Followers of Jesus is to discover and discern what he is already doing – 'for the Christ in me to meet the Christ in you' as the Celtic saints said. We try and keep an accurate perspective on who we are in God's big picture.

We believe the kingdom is greater than Church, but that where the kingdom of God is, Church happens. Our emphasis therefore is to seek to live kingdom lives focused on Jesus, rather than running around getting caught in all the trappings of Church. If all the people who meet Jesus through us are discipled through other churches in the area, we will be as happy as if they all came here.

We seek to do things *with* and not *for* people. Many people here are fed up with having things done for them, and the result is frequently a feeling of powerlessness and helplessness, an inability to change the status quo. Recently we have helped set up a management committee of local people which raised money to employ three workers to rebuild an adventure playground. Local people have seen how their contribution and skills can change something for the better.

When we started out, we wondered what name we should give this new church. A number of ideas were considered, but we decided it would be more appropriate to allow local people to name the church when they wanted to. When a couple of local guys started to follow Jesus, they asked why the church didn't have a name, and whether we could give it one. They were asked to think of a name themselves, and Cable Street Community Church was born. We named it with people, rather than impose what we thought best.

Finally, we seek to create households of believers on each estate. While large gatherings of Church are great, some aspects of Church are enhanced in a small-group setting. In a large church it is easy to hide and be less than real about one's life and walk with Jesus. In a small group relationships can become deeper, needs shared and responded to, and mission co-ordinated at a local, relational level. Those who have rejected Church can feel more comfortable, and those from another faith can find home gatherings more welcoming and open. As each of Shadwell's estates is different, we anticipate each household looking different. Church isn't monochrome.

The last five years have been an interesting, exciting, humbling, at times jubilant and at others heart-breaking journey. We look forward to what the next five will bring, and look to God to stir more people up with passion for urban ministry.

Questions for Further Thought and Action

1 To what extent are the principles identified by Urban Presence acted upon in and through your church? Use these as a check-list to evaluate your ministry.

2 How might the experience gained in this project be used in your setting? What are the ways your church or ministry could make contacts with people of other faith groups in sensitive ways?

3 Consider ways in which cell church could be used to develop in your situation. How might your church empower local people actually to do the pastoral care and evangelism themselves?

4 In what ways might the approach pioneered by Urban Expression be enacted in your locality? How can your church incarnate Christ in a way that is authentic to your wider community? Or do you need to set up a new 'congregation'?

Further Reading

1 Beginning to Think

The Story of Urban Mission in the UK (Colin Marchant)

Roger Dowley, *Towards the Recovery of the Lost Bequest* (ECUM, 1984).

Robert Linthicum, *City of God, City of Satan: A Biblical Theology of the Urban Church* (Zondervan, 1991).

Stuart Murray Williams, *City Vision: A Biblical View* (Darton, Longman & Todd, 1990).

Doing Theology in the Urban Context (Kenneth Leech)

Eric Blakebrough (ed.), *Church for the City* (Darton, Longman & Todd, 1995).

Kenneth Leech, *Through Our Long Exile: Contextual Theology and the Urban Experience* (Darton, Longman & Todd, 2001).

Robert J. Schreiter, *Constructing Local Theologies* (Orbis, 1993).

Key Biblical Themes (Colin Marchant)

Faith in the City (Church House Publishing, 1985).

Irene Howat and John Nicholls, *Streets Paved with Gold* (Christian Focus Publications, 2002).

Donald Lewis, *Lighten Their Darkness* (London City Mission, 2002).

2 Church Life

The Importance of Being Church (Steve Latham)

Ray Bakke, *The Urban Christian* (MARC, 1987).

Ray Bakke, *A Theology As Big As the City* (IVP, 1997).

Stanley Hauerwas and William H. Willimon, *Resident Aliens* (Abingdon Press, 1989).

Michael Northcott (ed.), *Urban Theology: A Reader* (Cassell, 1998).

Building a Community (Kofi Manful)

Colin Dye, *It's Time to Grow: Kick-starting a Church into Growth* (Harpenden, 1997).

Tom Marshall, *Right Relationships* (Sovereign World, 1992).

Local Church Leadership in Urban Communities (Jim Hart)
Laurie Green, *Let's Do Theology* (Mowbray, 1990).
Jonathan Rose, *The Intellectual Life of the British Working Classes* (Nota Bene, 2002).

New Models of Church (Stuart Murray Williams)
George Lings, *Encounters from the Edge* (from The Sheffield Centre, 50 Cavendish Street, Sheffield S3 7RZ).
Stuart Murray and Anne Wilkinson-Hayes, *Hope from the Margins* (Grove Books, 2000).

3 Spirituality and Worship

Maintaining Hope: How to Keep Going and Not Burn Out (Chris Burch)
Charles Elliott, *Praying the Kingdom* (Darton, Longman & Todd, 1985).
Gerard Hughes, *God of Surprises* (Darton, Longman & Todd, 1985).
Eric James (ed.), *Spirituality for Today* (SCM, 1968).
Kenneth Leech, *Soul Friend* (Sheldon, 1977).
John A. Sandford, *Ministry Burnout* (Arthur James, 1982).

Worship: Making it Real in the City? (Pete Hobson)
Pete Hobson, *Inner City Voices* (Scripture Union/CPAS, 1993).
C. S. Lewis, *Till We Have Faces* (Fount, 1998).

Urban Worship (Jacqueline Brown)
Colin Dye, *Building a City Church: The Kensington Temple Vision* (Dovewell/Kingsway, 1993).
Colin Dye, *Worship in Spirit and Truth: Sword of the Spirit 12* (Kensington Temple, 1999).

Worship Alternatives: Use of Arts and Creativity in Worship (Doug Gay)
Jonny Baker and Doug Gay, *Alternative Worship* (SPCK, 2003).
Pete Ward (ed.), *Mass Culture: Eucharist and Mission in a Post-Modern World* (The Bible Reading Fellowship, 1999).

4 Scripture

Bible Study: The Liberation Theology Method (John Vincent)
Leonardo Boff and Clodovis Boff, *Introducing Liberation Theology* (Burns & Oates, 1987).
C. Rowland and J. Vincent (eds), *Gospel from the City* (Urban Theology Unit, 1977).
John Vincent, *Hope From the City* (Epworth Press, 2000).
John Vincent (ed.), *Faithfulness in the City* (St Deiniol's Library, 2003).

Unlocking Real Life! (Jenny Richardson)
Paulo Freire, *Pedagogy of the Oppressed* (Penguin, 1972).
Laurie Green, *Let's Do Theology* (Mowbray, 1990).
David Kolb, 'The Process of Experiential Learning', in M. Thorpe, R. Edwards and A. Hanson (eds), *Culture and Processes of Adult Learning* (Open University Press, 1993).
Jenny Richardson, 'You Can Keep Your Hat On', in Chris Rowland and John Vincent, *The Bible in Practice* (Urban Theology Unit, 2001).
Jenny Richardson, 'Reading the Bible in the City: Urban Culture, Context and Interpretation', *Anvil*, Vol. 20, No. 1, 2003.

Preaching in an Urban World (Roger Sainsbury)
James H. Harris, *Preaching Liberation* (Fortress, 1995).
Olin Moyd, *The Sacred Art* (Judson Press, 1995).
Frank A. Thomas, *They Like to Never Quit Praisin' God* (United Church Press, 1997).
Walter Wink, *The Powers That Be* (Doubleday, 1998).

5 Community

Building Community: Within and Without the Walls of the Church (Greg Smith)
Z. Bauman, *Community: Seeking Safety in an Insecure World* (Polity Press, 2001).
E. M. Bounds, *Coming Together/Coming Apart: Religion, Community and Modernity* (Routledge, 1997).
G. Hillery, 'Definitions of Community; Areas of Agreement', *Rural Sociology* (1995).

Community Development (Chris Erskine)
David Oliver and James Thwaites, *Church That Works* (Word, 2001).
James Thwaites, *Renegotiating the Church Contract* (Paternoster, 2001).

'On' the Estate (Andy Dorton)
Laurie Green, *Power to the Powerless* (Marshalls, 1989).
Laurie Green, *The Challenge of the Estates: Strategies and Theology for Housing Estates Ministry* (Urban Bishops' Panel and National Estate Churches Network, 1999).
Michael Simmons (ed.), *Street Credo: Churches in the Community* (Lemon & Crane, 2000).

Political Involvement: Local Resistance to Regeneration Policies (Alan Craig)
Nile Harper, *Urban Churches: Beyond Charity Towards Justice* (Eerdmans, 1998).
Jim Wallis, *The Soul of Politics* (Fount, 1994).
Graham Ward, *Cities of God* (Routledge, 2000).

6 Race

The Multicultural Society, the Multicultural Church (Wale Hudson Roberts)
Robert Beckford, *Jesus is Dread: Black Theology and Culture in Britain* (Darton, Longman & Todd, 1998).
Kwesi Owusu, *Black British Culture and Society: A Text Reader* (Routledge, 2000).

'I Was a Stranger' (Sheila Garvin)
Andrew Bradstock and Arlington Trotman (eds), *Asylum Voices* (Council of Churches in Britain and Ireland, 2003).
Jeremy Harding, *The Uninvited: Refugees at the Rich Man's Gate* (Profile Books and The London Review of Books, 2000).
Jill Rutter and Crispin Jones (eds), *Refugee Education* (Trentham Books, 1998).

Look: A Multicultural Church! (Andy Bruce)
John Wilkinson, *The Church in Black and White* (St Andrews, 1994)

Planting a Chinese Congregation in Hounslow: A Decade of Mission (Robert Tang)
Roger Greenway, *Discipling the City* (Moody Press, 1999).
Manuel Ortiz and Susan Baker (eds), *The Urban Face of Mission* (Presbyterian and Reformed Publishing Company, 2002).

7 Cultural Change

Pluralism and Diversity (Graham Routley)
Les Black, *New Ethnicities and Urban Cultures* (UCL Press, 1996).
Lord Parekh, *The Future of Multi-Ethnic Britain* (Profile, 2000).

An Incomer's Tale (Mark Perrott)
R. Lewis, *The Church of Irresistible Influence* (Zondervan, 2002).
Ann Morisy, *Beyond the Good Samaritan: Community Ministry and Mission* (Mowbray, 1997).
J. Ortberg, *Everybody's Normal Till You Get to Know Them* (Zondervan, 2003).
G. Tomlin, *The Provocative Church* (SPCK, 2002).

Searching for Roots: Power and Powerlessness (Richard Springer)
Robert Beckford, *Dread and Pentecostal: A Political Theology for the Black Church in Britain* (SPCK, 2000).
Robert Beckford, *God of the Rahtid: Redeeming Rage* (Darton, Longman & Todd, 2001).
Jim Cummings, *Negotiating Identities: Education for Empowerment in a Diverse Society* (California Association for Bilingual Education, 1996).

Recent Arrivals (Wagih Abdelmassih)
Robin Cohen, *Global Diasporas: An Introduction* (University of Washington Press, 1997).
Andrew Davey, *Urban Christianity and Global Order: Theological Resources for an Urban Future* (SPCK, 2001).

8 Peace-making

The 174 Story (Patton Taylor)
Eoim Cassidy, Donal McKeown and John Morrow (eds), *Belfast: Faith in the City* (Veritas Publications, 2001).
Milbrey W. McLaughlin, Merita A. Irby and Juliet Langman, *Urban Sanctuaries: Neighbourhood Organizations and Futures of Inner City Youth* (Jossey-Bass, 1994).

Race in Northern Towns: Christian Responses to BNP–Muslim Tensions (Geoff Reid)
David Haslam, *Race for the Millennium* (Church House Publishing, 1996).
Kenneth Leech, *Struggle in Babylon* (Sheldon, 1989).

Gang Violence (Paul Keeble)
Mike Fearon, *With God on the Frontiers* (Scripture Union, 1988).
Edward Villafane, *Seek the Peace of the City* (Eerdmans, 1995).
Pip Wilson, *Gutter Feelings* (Marshall Pickering, 1985).

In the Congregation (Tim Foley)
Alan and Eleanor Kreider, *Becoming a Peace Church* (New Ground, 2000).
John Paul Lederach, *The Journey Toward Reconciliation* (Herald Press, 1999).
Carolyn Schrock-Shenk and Lawrence Ressler, *Making Peace with Conflict* (Herald Press, 1999).
Jim Stutzman and Carolyn Schrock-Shenk (eds), *Mediation and Facilitation Training Manual* (third edition) (Mennonite Conciliation Service, 1997).

9 Some Other Urban Issues

A Healthy Living Project in a Local Church (Simon Standen)
Fran Beckett, Steve Chalke *et al.*, *Rebuild: Small Groups Can Make a Difference* (Crossway Books, 2001).
Children and Social Exclusion (National Council of Voluntary Child Care Organisations, 1999).

Debt (Bob Holman)
Mary Beasley, *Mission on the Margins* (Lutterworth, 1997).
Bob Holman, *Towards Equality* (SPCK, 1997).

Elaine Kempson and Claire Whyley, *Kept Out or Opted Out? Understanding and Combatting Financial Exclusion* (Policy Press, 1999).

Work: Toxteth Tabernacle Baptist Church/Toxteth Vine Project (Terry Jones)
Nicholas Bradbury, *City of God: Pastoral Care in the Inner City* (SPCK, 1989).
Malcolm Grundy, *Light in the City: Stories of the Church Urban Fund* (Canterbury Press, 1990).
Jim Wallis, *Faithworks* (SPCK, 2002).

Employment (Dave Rogers)
John Atherton, *Marginalization* (SCM, 2003).
Unemployment and the Future of Work: An Enquiry for the Churches (Churches Together in Britain and Ireland, 1997).

10 Faith-Sharing

Urban Mission (Derek Purnell)
Harvie Conn, *Evangelism: Doing Justice and Preaching Grace* (Zondervan, 1982).
Harvey Conn and Manuel Ortiz, *Urban Ministry* (IVP, 2001).
David Sheppard, *Built as a City* (Hodder & Stoughton, 1974).

Evangelism in a Multifaith Setting (Amanda Gray)
Martin Goldsmith, *Islam and Christian Faith: Sharing the Faith with Muslims* (IVP, 1982).
Steven Masood, *Into the Light: A Young Muslim's Search for Truth* (Paternoster, 1986).
Kate Zebiri, *Muslims and Christians Face to Face* (One World Publications, 1997).

Urban Cell Church (Howard Astin)
Howard Astin, *Body and Cell: Making the Transition to Cell Church – A First-hand Account* (Monarch, 1998).
Laurence Singlehurst, *Loving the Lost: The Principles and Practice of Cell Church* (Kingsway, 2001.

Church Planting (Juliet Kilpin)
Harvie Conn (ed.), *Planting and Growing Urban Churches* (Baker Book House, 1997).
Stuart Murray Williams, *Church Planting: Laying Foundations* (Paternoster, 1998).

Urban Theology Unit
Pitsmoor Study House, 210 Abbeyfield Road, Sheffield S4 7AZ.
Phone: 0114 243 5342; fax: 0114 243 5356.
E-mail: office@utu-sheffield.demon.co.uk

National Estate Churches Network
C/o The Revd Andrew Davey, Church House, Great Smith Street, London
SW1P 3NZ.
Phone: 020 7898 1446; fax: 020 7898 1536.
E-mail: andrew.davey@c-of-e.org. uk

Churches' Commission for Racial Justice
Interchurch House, 35 Lower Marsh, London SE1 7RL.
Phone: 020 7654 7241; fax: 020 7654 7222.
E-mail: ccrj@ctbi.org.uk

South Asian Concern
50 Grove Road, Sutton, Surrey SM1 1BT.
Phone: 020 8770 9717; fax: 020 8770 9747.
E-mail: 100126.3641@compuserve.com

Alliance of Asian Christians
Carrs Lane Church Centre, Carrs Lane, Birmingham B4 7SX.
Phone: 0121 633 4533.
E-mail: 113402.3250@compuserve.com

African and Caribbean Evangelical Alliance
186 Kennington Park Road, London SE11 4BT.
Phone: 020 7735 7373
E-mail: acea@eauk.org

Inner Cities Religious Council
Department of the Environment, Transport and Regions, 4/J10 Eland House,
Bressenden Place, London SW1E 5DU.
Phone: 020 7944 3704; fax: 020 7944 3729.
E-mail: ICRC@detr.gov.uk

London Mennonite Centre
14 Shepherd's Hill, Highgate, London N6 5AQ.
Phone: 020 8340 8775; fax: 020 8341 6807.
E-mail: lmc@menno.org.uk

Frontier Youth Trust
Unit 2094, The Big Reg, 12 Vyse Street, Birmingham B18 6NF.
Phone: 0121 687 3505; fax: 0121 687 3506.
E-mail: frontier@tyt.org.uk; website: www.tyt.org.uk

Agencies, Networks and Resources

Evangelical Coalition for Urban Mission and **Network of Urban Evangelicals** (see page x), and **Urban Bulletin** (see page 4).

UK Urban Congress Trust
C/o Union Theological College, 108 Botanic Avenue, Belfast BT17 1JT.
Phone: 028 9020 5080; fax: 028 9020 5099.
E-mail: jp.taylor@union.ac.uk

Ecumenical Urban Officers Group
C/o The Revd Andrew Davey, Church House, Great Smith Street, Londc
SW1P 3NZ.
Phone: 020 7898 1446; fax: 020 7898 1536.
E-mail: andrew.davey@c-of-e.org.uk

Faith Works
The Oasis Centre, 115 Southwark Bridge Road, London SE1 0AX.
Phone: 020 7450 9000; fax: 020 7450 9001; website: www.faithworks.i
E-mail: info@faithworks.info

INCIT
179 Olive Mount Heights, Liverpool L15 8LD.

Urban Expression
PO Box 35238, London E1 4YA.
E-mail: www.urbanexpression.org.uk

Iona Community
Community House, Pearce Institute, 840 Govan Road, Glasgow G51 3U
Phone: 0141 332 6343; fax: 0141 382 1090.
E-mail: Ionacomm@iona.org.uk

Unlock
Unlock House, 336a City Road, Sheffield S2 1GA.
Phone: 0114 276 2038; fax: 0114 276 2035;
website: www.unlock-urban.org.uk
E-mail: office@unlock.force9.co.uk

Church Action on Poverty
Central Buildings, Oldham Street, Manchester M1 15T.
Phone: 0161 236 9321; fax: 0161 237 5359.
E-mail: info@church-poverty.org.uk

CURBS (Children in Urban Situations)
PO Box 344, Redhill RH1 3FG.
Phone: 01737 642522.
E-mail: info@curbsproject.org.uk; website: www.curbsproject.org.uk

Urban Presence
12 Morecambe Close, Newton Heath, Manchester M40 2FD.
Phone/fax: 0161 688 4789.
E-mail: derek@urbanpresence.org.uk

London City Mission
175 Tower Bridge Road, London SE1 2AH.
Phone: 020 7407 7585; fax: 020 7403 6711.
Website: www.lcm.org.uk